French Structuralism

Twayne's World Authors Series
French Literature

David O'Connell, Editor
Georgia State University

TWAS 818

French Structuralism

By Roland A. Champagne

University of Missouri-St. Louis

Twayne Publishers
A Division of G. K. Hall & Co. • Boston

French Structuralism
Roland A. Champagne

Copyright 1990 by G. K. Hall & Co.
All rights reserved.
Published by Twayne Publishers
A division of G. K. Hall & Co.
70 Lincoln Street, Boston, Massachusetts 02111

First Published 1990.
10 9 8 7 6 5 4 3 2 1

The paper used in this publication meets the minimum requirements
of American National Standard for Information Sciences—Permanence
of Paper for Printed Library Materials, ANSI Z39.48–1984. ∞™

Printed and bound in the United States of America

Library of Congress Cataloging in Publication Data

Champagne, Roland A.
    French structuralism / by Roland A. Champagne.
        p.   cm. — (Twayne's world authors series ; TWAS 818. French
    literature)
    Includes bibliographical references.
    ISBN 0-8057-8262-1 (alk. paper)
    1. Criticism—France—History—20th century.   2. French
literature—20th century—History and criticism—Theory, etc.
3. Structuralism (Literary analysis)   I. Title.   II. Series:
Twayne's world authors series ; TWAS 818.   III. Series: Twayne's
world authors series. French literature.
PQ79.C44   1990
801'.95'09440904—dc20   90-4210
                                                            CIP

à Noé
Noah's determined nature and his love of books have been a source
of inspiration for me during my weaker moments. To him, I dedicate this
work.

Contents

About the Author

Roland Champagne is professor of French at the University of Missouri-St. Louis. His research interests include the relationships among ideology, rhetoric, and psychology in twentieth-century literary theory. The author of previous books on Philippe Sollers, Julia Kristeva, Roland Barthes, and Claude Lévi-Strauss, he is now preparing a book on the French contextualist school of classical myth.

Preface

For the convenience of the reader in consulting the notes and references, I have tried to cite English-language editions whenever they are available. Likewise, in the selected bibliography, I have tried to choose English-language anthologies when available and well done to make it easier for those not familiar with French to consult these writers on their own. Whenever I did not cite a published translation but my own English version, I am responsible for the resulting "treachery" from one language to the other. Because of the disparity in time and in sense between the appearance of French structuralism and its debate today, I decided to use the past tense of verbs to indicate what happened in the development of French structuralism and the present tense to discuss the published writings of the individuals as they speak to us today.

Once again, I thank Hugh M. Davidson and Charles G. S. Williams for introducing me to the joys of Roland Barthes's writings as my entry into French structuralism. From there, Nina Ekstein guided me with her unpublished essay on Goldmann, Brian Vandenberg oriented me in genetic structuralism with his insights into Piaget, and Willis Salomon kept me thinking, during our long discussions of Habermas and Cavell, about the Hegelian nature of the French structuralists.

Roland A. Champagne

University of Missouri-St. Louis

Chronology

1759   Voltaire satirizes the optimism of monadology in his *Candide*.

1860–1865   Herbert Spencer applies the "structure" of biological organisms to social entities.

1907   Ferdinand de Saussure gives the first of his three lectures on linguistics, the basis for his *Cours de linguistique générale*.

1912   Saussure's students—Bally, Sechehaye, and Riedlinger—have their notes published as Saussure's *Cours de linguistique générale*.

1925   Marcel Mauss's *Essai sur le don* is published.

1926   Prague Linguistic Circle is founded by Roman Jakobson and colleagues.

1927   Martin Heidegger publishes *Sein und Zeit* (*Being and Time*).

1928   Vladimir Propp's *Morphology of the Folktale* is published.

1929   Marc Bloch and Lucien Febvre establish the *Annales* School of history.

1933   Léa and Christine Papin, kitchen maids, murder their mistresses. N. S. Troubetzkoy's *Psychologie du langage* introduces phonology.

1936   Jacques Lacan presents "Le Stade du Miroir" to the International Psychoanalytical Congress in Marienbad.

1939   Emile Benveniste's *Nature du signe linguistique* is published.

1941   Roman Jakobson and Claude Lévi-Strauss meet at the New School for Social Research in New York City.

1943   Louis Hjelmslev's *Prolegomena to a Theory of Language* introduces glossematics.

1948   Louis Althusser, at age thirty, joins the Communist Party.

1953   Jacques Lacan's "Discours de Rome" generates a split between the Paris and the International Psychoanalytic Associations.

1955   Lucien Goldmann's *Le Dieu caché* is published.

1956   Jacques Lacan begins his seminars.

1957   Roland Barthes's *Mythologies* is published as a book.

1958   Claude Lévi-Strauss's *Tristes Tropiques* and volume 1 of his *Anthropologie structurale* are published. Charles de Gaulle's Fifth Republic is acknowledged by the French National Assembly.

1959   Martin Heidegger publishes *Unterwegs zur Sprache* (*On the Way to Language*), thus making the case for the linguistic "turn" in his philosophy.

1960   Louis Althusser's "Sur le Jeune Marx" is published in *La Pensée*. Lévi-Strauss gives his inaugural lecture for his election to the Collège de France. André Martinet's *Eléments de linguistique générale* is published. Philippe Sollers and colleagues begin editing the journal *Tel Quel* at the publisher Seuil. French intellectuals sign the "Manifesto of the 121" protesting the Algerian War.

1961   Michael Foucault's *L'Histoire de la folie à l'âge classique* is published.

1962   Jakobson and Lévi-Strauss's reading of Baudelaire's "Les Chats" is published in *L'Homme*.

1963   Publication of Jakobson's *Essai de linguistique générale*, Lévi-Strauss's *Le Totemisme aujourd'hui* and his *La Pensée sauvage*, and Roland Barthes's *Sur Racine*.

1964   Publication of Roland Barthes's *Essais critiques* and volume 1 of Lévi-Strauss's *Mythologiques*. Lacan is expelled from the International Psychoanalytic Association.

1965   Publication of Althusser's *Pour Marx* and his and E. Balibar's *Lire le Capital* and Raymond Picard's *Nouvelle Critique ou nouvelle imposture?* Althusser becomes editor of "Collection Théorie" for the publisher Maspero.

1966   Publication of Barthes's *Critique et vérité*, Foucault's *Les Mots et les choses*, A. J. Greimas's *Sémantique structurale*, Lacan's *Écrits*, and Pierre Macherey's *Pour une théorie de la production littéraire*. Johns Hopkins University sponsors a conference on the Languages of Criticism and the Sciences of Man in Baltimore.

1967   Publication of Jacques Derrida's *De la Grammatologie*,

L'Écriture et la différence, and *La Voix et le phénomène* as well as Rudolf Engler's critical edition of Saussure's *Cours* with student notes.

1968   May revolts by students and workers in Paris. Publication of Althusser's *Lenine et la philosophie,* Gilles Deleuze's *La Différence et la répétition,* and Jean Piaget's *Le Structuralisme.* Jean Pierre Faye organizes the *Change* Collectif and edits the first issue of *Change.* First issue appears of *Scilicet,* a review publishing Lacan's lectures on "Le Champ freudien." Vincennes campus of the University of Paris becomes the site for reforms in French education. Foucault becomes chair of the Vincennes Department of Philosophy.

1969   DeGaulle resigns as Président de la République. Althusser calls for an end to "Althusserianism." Deleuze's *Logique du sens* is published. Foucault is elected to the Collège de France.

1970   Foucault's inaugural lecture to the Collège de France is published as *L'Ordre du discours.*

1972   John Lewis's "The Case of Althusser" is published in *Marxism Today.* Tzvetan Todorov and Oswald Ducrot's *Dictionnaire encyclopédique des sciences du langage,* Deleuze and Félix Guattari's *L'Anti-Oedipe,* and René Girard's *La Violence et le sacré* are published.

1973   Althusser's *Réponse à John Lewis* is published.

1974   Althusser's *Éléments d'Auto-Critique* is published.

1975–1981   Lacan is director of journal *Ornicar?,* published by the Department of Psychoanalysis, University of Paris—VIII, Sorbonne.

1977   Barthes is elected to the Collège de France. Todorov's *Théories des symboles* is published.

1980   President of France Giscard d'Estaing has the Vincennes campus of the University of Paris bulldozed. Lacan dissolves the École Freudienne de Paris.

1981   Todorov's *Mikhail Bakhtine: Le principe dialogique* is published.

1984   Todorov's *Critique de la critique* is published.

Chapter One

The French in Structuralism

The French contributed philosophical, psycholinguistic, and mathematical models for the establishment of a structuralist intellectual climate, an ideology, and a method. The word *structuralism* has often been identified with a group of French writers whose singularity of purpose and resulting effects were not obviously singular. Although Claude Lévi-Strauss (b. 1908), Roland Barthes (1915–80), Jacques Lacan (1901–81), Michel Foucault (1926–84), and Louis Althusser (b. 1918) were often brought together under the same rubric as French structuralists, their heterogeneous intentions and individual achievements far outweigh their reduction to a common way of looking at humanity and the world. Lévi-Strauss[1] and Foucault[2] vigorously rejected this association during the latter stages of their publishing careers. And yet, despite themselves, the work of these five writers carried on an intellectual heritage that is now being assimilated and developed in the research of semioticians throughout the world. French structuralism made its presence known primarily through the theories advanced by these five writers and then secondarily through others inspired by their work to take these theories beyond their inherent limitations.

It now behooves us to review the intellectual heritage of structuralism from the perspective of semiotics. As the science of communication, semiotics provides a wider context than language models within which to present the stakes, limitations, and accomplishments of structuralism. In addition, structuralism was an international literary, philosophical, and methodological enterprise. The French notwithstanding, various groups and individuals from many other cultures have contributed to the evolution of structuralism. We can isolate the Swiss students of Ferdinand de Saussure (1857–1913), the Prague Circle according to Roman Jakobson (1896–1982) and the Russian formalists by association, the Danish School of Louis Hjelmslev (1899–1965), and the American students of Leonard Bloomfield (1887–1949) as the major clusters of structuralist influence. I provide a general overview of these schools as distinct from the French variant and as part of an international raising of consciousness that views linguistics as a discipline having much to offer the modern world.

Some readers may say, "Oh, no, not another book on structuralism," just when we thought that Jonathan Culler's *Structuralist Poetics* had given us the definitive view of structuralist parameters and issues. However, Frank Lentricchia revealed the limitations of a "structuralist poetics" as a theoretical oxymoron.[3] Culler told us that the theories of Noam Chomsky (b. 1928) could provide a map for the heterogeneous directions of structural linguistics.[4] But Chomsky's linguistic program was in response to the American behavioral orientation of the Bloomfield structuralists and is incongruous with the French program for structuralism. My purpose here is to differentiate the French variant from other types of structuralism and to discuss the voices of French structuralism as distinct within this pluralistic historical phenomenon.

The heyday of the French variant of structuralism can be pinpointed as the decade 1958 to 1968, these limits being marked off by the respective publications of *Anthropologie structurale* by Claude Lévi-Strauss and *Le Structuralisme* by Jean Piaget (1896–1980). Lévi-Strauss called popular attention to the ethnological applications of structural linguistics and heralded a period of major intellectual creativity. Philosophically, Martin Heidegger's *Being and Time*, published in 1927, was the rage in France due to Jean-Paul Sartre's existential presentation of its message. In 1959, Heidegger (1889–1976) published *On the Way to Language*, which announced a linguistic "turn" in his philosophy, thus attracting attention to structuralism "as a serious philosophical counterpart to existentialism." In 1968, Piaget signaled the death knell of French structuralism by specifying its scientific and positivistic claims on truth and method. In reaction to Piaget's little treatise, the philosophical excitement about the avant-garde possibilities for structuralism began to wane in France. Many intellectuals in other cultures, however, have continued to discover structuralism and to apply its principles.

I have developed elsewhere[5] the case for structuralism as a pluralistic phenomenon in that many theoreticians have laid claim to what it was. *Structuralism* has been used to identify various methods and perspectives, whereas in Paris the word became fashionable[6] in philosophical and literary circles. Basically, a critical mass, in the physicists' sense, developed in France about forty years after the 1912 publication of Ferdinand de Saussure's lectures on linguistics at the University of Geneva. No single ideology resulted from the many strands woven into the fabric of this French version of structuralism. But it was clearly an intellectual event of major proportions whose "French" character was shaped by natives of many countries other than France. This version is called "French" by reference to the locus of Paris, where many of the exponents of structuralism who wrote principally in French were published, and their works promoted as French. Let us first examine the character and history of structuralism, then its bases in philosophy, psycholinguistics, and mathematics, and finally the ideologies and intellectual climate fostered by its evolution and melding into semiotics, deconstruction, and other, still developing theories.

What Is a Structure?

The word *structure* is derived from the Latin etymon *struere* meaning "to build" and "structura" signifying "building." The etymons as verb and noun are important for the debate within structuralism between "structure" and "structuring" as the primary focus of the methodology.[7] Within the context of the philosophical attitude called structuralism, the "building" refers to a skeleton or form whose exact shape and constituents are not obvious to the observer. The "structure" is usually hidden from view and entails connections beneath the surface among often apparently heterogeneous concerns.

Generally, the term was adapted from the sciences in the nineteenth century, especially from biology whereby genetic coding provided a model for the social sciences and the humanities. In *Being and Time*, Heidegger spoke of the "structure of care" whereby Being (*Dasein*) was the focus for ontological reflection in a philosophy without metaphysics. Metaphysics had failed to ask the question of how the essence of humanity was related structurally to the truth of Being. Heidegger proposed that philosophy address the question of structure or cease to exist. In the field of psychology, Jean Piaget adapted the scientific method to understand "structure" as the genesis of cognitive stages of development. The word *genesis*, however, is a bit misleading because Piaget had a very limited sense of history. For his structures, history constituted a cause-and-effect relationship in which mystery, morality, and human care were excluded as too playful within the context of verifiable parameters. Likewise, other early studies of structure were developed in contradistinction to historical explanations of phenomena.

Within the social and human science milieux in general, the very definition of *structure* was a rhetorical exercise. Just as the medieval study of rhetoric entailed grammar, dialectics, and mathematics, so the French evolution of structuralism could be divided into a similar rhetorical trivium. In this vein, the French theoretician Jean-Marie Benoist described "the structuralist revolution"[8] as having three components: linguistics, philosophy, and mathematics. I generally agree with Benoist but modify linguistics as psycholinguistics because of the impact of psychological studies through the intervention of

Piaget, Jacques Lacan, and Roland Barthes. In addition, I prefer ideology to philosophy because of the lack of conscious association by many French philosophers with the "structuralist" label.

These three fields were subdivisions of rhetoric. The reason is that French structuralism was centered in Paris where fashion and influence invoke a unique form of snobbery, and rhetoric has been the vehicle for dominating this scene since the twelfth century and Abelard. During the heyday of structuralism from 1958 to 1968, the jargon and terminology associated with a "structure" set it off against history so that structuralism was clearly opposed to existentialism, especially the Sartrean variant with so much emphasis on historical good faith and commitment. Claude Lévi-Strauss returned from his exile in the United States with ahistorical stories from Brazilian and American Indian tribes that fascinated his French readers. He had been influenced by Roman Jakobson's Prague Circle linguistics and had adapted the set theories of the French Bourbaki mathematics from the 1930s. Thus structure became a way to assimilate the myths or stories of these remote cultures.

Émile Benveniste (1902–76), a French linguist, noted that structure was an arrangement of a whole whose parts were demonstrably coherent and reciprocal.[9] The "arrangement of wholes" was a key concept that served to irritate Jean-Paul Sartre (1905–80) because structuralism was thus an anticausal orientation, denying historical contexts for its argumentation. It was anticausal in that abstract ensembles and connections were sought rather than specific "chronotopes" (*sic* Bakhtin)[10] linking phenomena with the milieu of a given moment. Instead of a chronological or horizontal explanation, a vertical or relational perspective opened with the employment of structures in the social sciences and the humanities.

The structure was often allied with "system" as the tapestry of structuralism was woven. Structuralism was an approach, a method rather than a program of philosophical tenets. In the evolution of this method linking structure within a larger order called a system, there is a clear split between the Yale School begun by Leonard Bloomfield in the 1930s and the French structuralists. The Yale School understood system as classification, whereas the French preferred system as an overarching whole within which a structure had a context.

On the one hand, Bloomfield (*Language*, 1933) understood structure as a category, a niche in which to classify phenomena and to determine the basic units of language. Zellig S. Harris (b. 1909) continued the work of Bloomfield and was the mentor of the transformational grammarian Noam Chomsky. Chomsky's distinctions between competence and performance are hallmarks in the history of structuralism, as is elaborated in Culler's, *Structuralist Poetics*. Justin Lieber, in an earlier Twayne volume on structuralism, noted that structural linguistics has a bias for the physical against the intellectual in its work[11]; he was speaking about Bloomfield's Yale School of structuralism.

On the other hand, the French structuralists were much more concerned with abstract wholes rather than with the elements themselves. N. S. Troubetzkoy (1890–1938) discovered phonemes, sound units regulated by the laws of the structure in which they are members. Although both Troubetzkoy and Bloomfield were doing research on sound structures, they had very different ideological orientations. Whereas the Yale School was concerned with taxonomies and atomistic theories of sound construction without reference to either meaning or a theory of relations, the Prague (of which Troubetzkoy was a member) and the French Schools focused on the relationships of the parts to the whole. Early in 1958, Claude Flament stated the typical French position by defining structure as an ensemble of elements related in such a way that any change in one relationship would entail changes in the other connections.[12] In other words, the French were more intent on studying the abstract relationships of a structure than on examining taxonomies. When the French were concerned with classification, they were more interested in the overview than in the actual application.[13] Of course, there were exceptions (see chapter 8, on the search for a universal grammar). Tzvetan Todorov (b. 1939), a Bulgarian who published his major structuralist works in French, is a notable exception. His attention to detail is admired by many Anglo-Saxons trained in empirical methods of scholarship.

The Swiss linguist Ferdinand de Saussure is the direct and indirect source for much of the theorizing about structure among the French. Aside from the publication of his writings in the French language, the reason for this is that language studies, especially the kind developed in linguistics, verified the philosophical and mathematical findings about the nature of the phenomenon called structure. Émile Benveniste, whose linguistic theories have elaborated Saussure's arguments, noted that language is a system in which no single element possesses meaning in itself but that the pattern of elements creates meaning.[14] The psychological model of the gestalt, with its holistic network of relations, retrieved the romantic notion of organic unity and was akin to Saussure's "system" for language. Similarly, there were philosophical and scientific precedents upon which Saussure based his theories of language. Let us first look at the development of events, leading up to and beyond Saussure, into what became known as French structuralism.

A Philosophy or an Ideology?

Baron Gottfried Leibnitz (1646–1716) provided the first thorough view of the universe as a structured whole. On a diplomatic mission in France, he met Antoine Arnauld in Paris and learned a universal calculus for "monadology." The Leibnitzian combination of mathematics and philosophy influenced the French considerably, as Voltaire satirized the optimism in the system with *Candide* in 1759 and other *philosophes* were influenced by the scientific analyses ensuing from the harmonic theories of the monads. Of course, the pre-Socratic Greek philosophers Pythagoras and Democritus had postulated harmonic conversion and atomism much earlier than Leibnitz. Monadology, as conceived by Leibnitz, assumed a preestablished harmony in the universe and a congruency among the basic units or elements of the harmony called monads. Although Leibnitz would have too optimistic a setting for a harmony in which God was the ultimate monad, monadology offered a model for scientific analysis whereby the organizational scaffolding of the world could be revealed. Indeed, the weltanschauung invented by Leibnitz was so pervasive that Jean-Marie Benoist saw French structuralism in 1975 as having reinvented "a Leibnitzian era."[15]

Leibnitz's work was not appreciated fully by the French until the nineteenth century. Monadology was understood as too optimistic and theistic for the Enlightenment. During this period the word *structure* was used in the sciences independently of any humanistic or social worldview. According to Lévi-Strauss, the Englishman Herbert Spencer (1820–1903) is the "forgotten father"[16] of the term *structure*. Spencer borrowed from biology the distinction between function and structure and applied it to social organisms during the period 1860–65. Along with Auguste Comte (1798–1857), the founder of modern sociology, Spencer theorized that all societies pass through the same evolutionary stages, from savagery to barbarism to civilization. He focused debates on whether there could be a common structure linking human societies in disparate geographical regions.

The young discipline of psychology also provided input for this debate. The psyche or soul could possibly be a structure uniting humanity. Franz Brentano (1837–1917) and the Gestalt psychologists Wolfgang Köhler (1887–1967) and Max Wertheimer (1880–1943) theorized about the mental networks of sensory data. There were two tendencies here that would become important as the diametrical principles separating the Yale and the French schools. On the one hand, the Gestalt psychologists were more interested in patterns created by the mind as it organized sense-data than in changes in the data or the influence of parts on the whole. The "gestalt" was more than the sum of its parts. Hence, there was little interest in the influences of the parts on the whole.

Brentano, on the other hand, invented a "descriptive psychology" that would deal with the parts. He distinguished methodologically between genetic psychology, concerned with the origins of psychic behavior, and his descriptive psychology, intent on narrating what is there. This distinction would have strong ramifications for the Prague Circle, especially in the founding of phonology.[17] It was in 1905 when Brentano observed that "individual sounds and even combinations of sounds which make up words have no meaning of themselves and often they are signs of a multiplicity of thoughts."[18] There is a direct philosophical link from this observation to Saussure's courses in Geneva to Roman Jakobson's poetics to Troubetzkoy's invention of the field of phonology, the study of sounds and meaning.

Of course, "philosophy" is too organized a perspective for uniting these heterogeneous voices that became the precursors of structuralism. From Democritus and Pythagoras to Brentano, there was a sensibility for a network of elements providing a unity of perspective for seemingly unconnected phenomena. These various voices did not act in unison nor in collaboration on what the network was. By focusing on language, Ferdinand de Saussure finally provided the vision for an ideology of structure founded in research on human communication. Language offered the promise of uniting ideas, phenomena, and words in a single object of study. But Lévi-Strauss was joined by Roland Barthes in objecting to a philosophy, a systematizing of this work on structures. Barthes preferred that structuralism be known as "an activity . . . beyond philosophy."[19] That activity began with linguistics and psychology, two disciplines in their infancy in the early twentieth century.

Psycholinguistic Modeling

Many believe that structural linguistics has so dominated structuralism that the structuralist tone and methodology are uniquely linguistic. We must bear in mind, however, that psychology and linguistics were evolving at about the same time during the nineteenth century. Darwin's dramatic case for evolution was modeled by genetic psychologists and "neogrammarian" linguists searching for etymons. The linguists of the period were influenced in various ways by their colleagues in psychology such that French structuralists would place René Descartes and his proposal of the body-mind dichotomy at the heart of their debates. Epistemology, as the discipline studying the generation of knowledge, would become the focal point for several linguistic schools emerging in the early twentieth century. The Geneva School and Saussure, the Prague Circle and Jakobson, and the Copenhagen School and Hjelmslev, contrasted by the Yale School and Bloomfield, would all form clusters of influence crucial in the development of French structuralism. Let us examine the specific stakes in the formation of these schools.

The Geneva School   Ferdinand de Saussure is actually a fictional character in the story of structuralism. His classic *Cours de linguistique générale* appeared in 1916 after his death. We know that he delivered lectures on the subject at the University of Geneva from 1906–11 and that the work we ascribe to him was edited by two colleagues, Charles Bally (1865–1947) and Albert Sechehaye (1870–1946), and a student, Albert Riedlinger. A critical edition now exists, with student notes from the three Saussure lectures, none of which Bally and Sechehaye attended.[20] In fact, the Saussure of the *Cours* may never have existed except as he was recreated through the editions of his notes.[21]

Nevertheless, as a practical matter the publication of the *Cours* influenced three generations of intellectuals in the formation of structuralism. The *Cours* was widely read by influential linguists such as Roman Jakobson, Louis Hjelmslev, and Leonard Bloomfield. The erudition of these three individuals led to the formation of linguistic circles around them, in Prague, Copenhagen, and New Haven, respectively. The Prague and Copenhagen schools had a direct influence on French structuralists. But the Yale (New Haven) School evolved concomitantly through Noam Chomsky's transformational grammar into a group of deconstructionists on the heels of Jacques Derrida (b. 1930), in the early 1980s.

The Prague and Copenhagen schools of linguistics were especially influential through the works of Émile Benveniste and A. J. Greimas (b. 1917). The major link, however, is between Prague Circle founder Roman Jakobson and Belgian-born ethnologist Claude Lévi-Strauss in New York during the early 1940s. Then and there was French structuralism founded, as Jakobson shared the lessons of structural linguistics, gleaned from Saussure's notes, with Lévi-Strauss. Ethnology has never been the same, because of the seminal work by this team and the consequent applications of linguistics during the 1950s and 1960s by Lévi-Strauss.

Let us return to the heritage of the Geneva School, usually known as the teachings of Saussure. In the notes to his courses, biology is acknowledged as the forerunner of his type of linguistics. During the nineteenth century, Darwin and his successors had provided biology with the model for many of the newly founded social sciences (psychology, sociology, linguistics). The concept of evolution brought about a heightened awareness of a system underlying the apparent heterogeneity of data. Similar to Brentano's theories about the arbitrary relationship between grammatical system and meaning,[22] Saussure's scheme mapped out language by sketching the interdependence of meaning and system. Indeed, Piaget would reiterate some fifty years later that Saussure's primary contribution was to point out the importance of the systemic map of structure.[23] That map began with the psychological observation that language structure is manifested in the consciousness of the speech community. This remark spawned the distinction between the individual use of language (*parole*) and the "grammatical system which, to all intents and purposes, exists in the mind of each speaker" (*langue*).[24] It is the positioning of the individual use, within the system of language, that determines meaning.

As opposed to the neogrammarian linguists of the nineteenth century who were concerned with the history of language, the Geneva group advocated a distinction between the historical (diachronic) and the contemporary (synchronic) studies of language. The *Cours* theorized about the nature of the synchronic study of language while a contemporary phonologist in Kazan, Russia, Jan Baudouin de Courtenay (1845–1929), had already broken from the influence of the neogrammarians to present the function of sounds in the grammatical and lexical system of a language.[25] And once the distinction between diachronic and synchronic was made, it would become very difficult, as Fredric Jameson has noted, to put them back together again.[26]

The *Cours* would have us believe that semiology, the French word for semiotics (the science of signs), is the system incorporating the structures of language. But in his later, unpublished study of anagrams among the Latin poets, Saussure inverted the relationship of language and semiology. The debate about which is the system incorporating the other continued throughout the history of French structuralism. According to the science of semiotics today, semiology receives the nod, in that signs are more broadly interpreted than words even though words constitute the primary system of communication known to humanity. Nevertheless, Saussure's *Cours* stresses the bifurcations within language rather than the modeling of language on semiology.

The sign itself was described in the *Cours* as having an arbitrary meaning linking the components of the signifier (*signifiant*) with the signified (*signifié*). Albert Sechehaye probed the disparity between these two major constituents of the sign. He separated phonemes from grammatical layers, thus corroborating Troubetzkoy's claim for a separate discipline of phonology: "Phonology should investigate which phonic differences are linked, in the language under consideration, with differences of meaning, how these differentiating elements or marks are related to one another, and according to what rules they combine to form words and phrases."[27] As with the separation of synchrony and diachrony, once the separation was discerned between the signifier and the signified, there was no turning back to a prior understanding. The arbitrary assignment of meaning to sounds would have reverberations far beyond the disciplinary discussions in linguistics.

The *Cours* notes that "thought, chaotic by nature, has to become ordered in the process of its decomposition."[28] And so the Geneva School set up the agenda for structuralism: to discover the hidden order in human thought. The theoretical distinctions of the unmotivated, arbitrary nature of the sign and the bifurcations of langue/parole, synchrony/diachrony, and signifier/signified constitute seminal ideas for stimulating additional discoveries. Roman Jakobson, a Russian who immigrated to Czechoslovakia, was a crucial link in the development of these ideas.[29]

The Prague Circle   The Prague Circle or School was organized in 1926 by Jakobson, Vilem Mathesius, Bohuslav Havranek, Jan Mukarovsky, and Bohumil Trnka. They would become distinguished for their phonological studies and their "functional linguistics." This latter term was invented because the Circle's published agenda in 1929 focused on the conception of language as a functional system largely conditioned by external, nonlinguistic factors.[30] And yet Trnka could identify structuralism as a distinct activity because it is "the trend of linguistics which is concerned with analysing relationships between the segments of a language, conceived as a hierarchically arranged whole."[31]

So structuralism was a specific interest of the Prague Circle but not the only focus of its agenda, as the Praguists reiterated that synchronic description would not in itself preclude the notion of linguistic evolution. Lévi-Strauss would later insist upon the incompatibility of history and structuralism. But the Prague Circle did not intend in its program to construct an intellectual barrier between synchrony and diachrony.

Once again, Franz Brentano had a significant influence. His distinction between genetic and descriptive psychology was crucial for the task of the Praguists. Some would even say that the Circle inherited its methodology from Brentano.[32] Nevertheless, the Praguist orientation was to promote the investigation of linguistic typology. We have already mentioned the founding of phonology by a later member of the Circle, N. S. Troubetzkoy, in 1933 with his *Psychologie du langage*. In the Prague Circle, the problem of "language alliance" was first identified. This is called *Sprachbund* (speech bundle) and is the phenomenon whereby languages share similar features even though they are unrelated historically. Hence, the synchrony of the Geneva

School came into play and would eventually lead to the Lévi-Strauss proposal of a "universal spirit" for all human thinking.

Of the Prague group, Roman Jakobson's research has had the most lasting impact on French structuralism. As early as 1929 he noted that structuralism was "the leading idea in present-day science in its most various manifestations."[33] His contributions are complex and substantial in the development of structural linguistics and its relationships to literary studies. Inspired by the bifurcations of the Geneva School and Troubetzkoy's theory of phonemic oppositions (marked versus unmarked phonological features), Jakobson implemented a binary orientation inherited by Lévi-Strauss in his adaptation of structural linguistics in ethnology.

Jakobson defined distinctive features as sound properties differentiating phonemes from each other, in which each phoneme is a bundle of these distinctive features. André Martinet (b. 1908), a French structural linguist, portrayed the phoneme as struggling within language between the poles of communicating with others and economizing physical and mental energy.[34] This semiotic tension had been characterized by Jakobson as a "poetic" contention. His dense aphorism about the poetic function is now classic Jakobson: "The poetic function projects the principle of equivalence from the axis of selection into the axis of combination."[35] Basically, these axes revealed the dichotomy between difference and similarity.

Indeed, the two axes of poetic functioning set up the dichotomies for his controversial analysis of Charles Baudelaire's poem "Les Chats" (The cats) (*L'Homme*, 2:1962).[36] He and Lévi-Strauss combined their talents to apply this structuralist analysis to a literary document. Theirs is a curious work: one that invited intellectuals to reply in anger at first and to recommend that the structural linguists leave literary criticism to the professionals.[37] Nevertheless, the effort was an interdisciplinary attempt to combine phonology, ethnology, and literary theory to show the world that structuralism was not simply a debatable topic within linguistics.

Jakobson brought his linguistic skills to the New School for Social Science Research in New York during the 1930s. He organized a society in structural linguistics there and founded the journal *Word*. In 1941, Lévi-Strauss joined Jakobson in New York and published some of his first pieces applying structural linguistics in this journal. Through Jakobson's influence on Lévi-Strauss, French structuralism would be permanently marked by Jakobson's agenda for structuralism: "Any set of phenomena examined by contemporary science is treated not as a mechanical agglomeration but as a structural whole, and the basic task is to reveal the inner, whether static or developmental, laws of this system."[38] Born in Moscow, Jakobson had natural ties to the formalist scholars in Russia who were doing theoretical research about the nature of the "laws of this system." It is these formalists whom I will discuss for insights into what Jakobson meant by the phenomena of structuralism.

Russian Formalism   Jakobson would pave the way for contemporary semiotics by encouraging interdisciplinary examinations of the functioning of language. He identified six factors involved in communication that still constitute a model for structuralist analysis: the message, the addresser, the addressee, the context, the code, and the method of contact. The model is a poetic one being examined by those concerned with "narratology," a science of the narrative. Gérard Genette, Gerald Prince, Teun van Dijk, and Tzvetan Todorov are among the chief delineators of this poetics, to be discussed in chapter 8.

Todorov is especially important for bringing Jakobson's work to the attention of the French in an anthology of the Russian formalists (*Théorie de la littérature*, 1965). Todorov also included selections translated into French from Russian by Chklovski, Propp, Tomachevski, and Khlebnikov. Todorov's amalgamation of their theories about the formal integrity of literary works is an important contribution to aesthetics by French structuralism. Todorov's *Critique de la critique* (1984) is now translated into English (*Literature and Its Theorists*, 1986) and provides an important assessment of the Soviet and French contributors to a poetics. From the Paris-based CNRS (Centre National de la Recherche Scientifique), Todorov has launched a campaign to develop a *poïétique*[39] incorporating formalist and structuralist theories.

Vladimir Propp's analysis of Russian folktales, *The Morphology of the Folktale,* originally published in 1928, has been cited as a precursor to French structuralism. Propp's apparent rejection of historical explanations in favor of an internal analysis seemed similar to the stance taken by Lévi-Strauss. Propp also wrote an introduction to the French translation of his book and used the opportunity to distinguish form from structure. His argument was that structure could include form and content whereas form was restricted to the medium of a given communication. However, Propp's work has been admired by other French structuralists, notably A. J. Greimas, whose analyses I will present later in this chapter, in elaborating on the influence of the Copenhagen School and Hjelmslev.

The theories of Jurij Lotman (b. 1922) have also received quite a bit of attention in France. His work has been translated into French and has received some accolades from those who are concerned with ideology and culture[40] as these are encrypted in texts. These "texts" are units of communication and can be as diverse as films analyzed by Christian Metz or Claude Chabrol. Jean Pierre Faye (b. 1925) especially publicized Lotman's ideas, in the journal *Change*, first published in Paris in 1968 as a reaction to *Tel Quel*, a journal begun in 1960 by Philippe Sollers (b. 1936) and others as a vehicle of the "structuralist" avant-garde.[41] Lotman was the director of the Tartu School of Semiotics, which investigated the role of culture as a plurality of interacting and mutually supportive sign systems. His theories will probably receive more attention in a poststructuralist environment, in which semiotics becomes a legitimized academic pursuit throughout the world.

The work of Mikhail Bakhtin (1895–1975) has become especially popular in the poststructuralist era. Julia Kristeva (b. 1941), after emigrating from Bulgaria and joining the *Tel Quel* group in 1967, promoted Bakhtin's literary theories as she developed her own theory of intertextuality to expand the limited focus that structuralism had given to the word "text."

Bakhtin rejected the Soviet structuralist agenda, and his analysis of Rabelais (*Rabelais and His World*, 1968) gave the French a model for reintegrating history with the synchronic studies becoming so fashionable. He theorized that any utterance is composed of voices and decipherable according to a "chronotope," historical information that lends especially incisive and insightful readings to a communication.

Many of the Russian formalists—such as Tynianov, Tomachevsky, Uspenskii, Eichenbaum, Brik, and Khlebnikov—have had a limited effect on the French structuralists. The formalist influence is limited to individual situations. For example, Tynianov's theories about the serial nature of narratives are crucial to Gilles Deleuze's philosophical treatise on narrative logic, *Logique du Sens* (The logic of meaning). I refer you to Matejka and Baran's anthologies of these writers for more details about their specific theories. In general, the Russian formalists provided poetic models for the French structuralists to modify their stance on structure. The word *form* would generate considerable debate among those who perceived themselves as "structuralist" in orientation. The Copenhagen School, with Hjelmslev at the helm, helped to clarify what constituted form.

The Copenhagen School Louis Hjelmslev augmented the theories of Saussure's *Cours* and elaborated a context for discussing the form of a structure. Whereas Jakobson and the formalists focused on poetic models, Hjelmslev offered a semiological model of communication with a "logical grammar" or algebra as a prototype. Language is not the ultimate or only model by which we communicate. This semiotic (rather than linguistic) theory is known as *glossematics*.

In 1943, Hjelmslev distinguished between form and substance, expression and content. On the one hand, form is a mental construct while substance is a physical representation of the mental construct. On the other hand, content is what is communicated while expression is how something is communicated. By making these distinctions, he outlined the scope of glossematics: to study the relationship between the form of the expression and the form of the content. Thus, he identified the Copenhagen School as formalist, in the strict sense in which he understood "form." Linguistics thus entered into the realm of epistemology, where it was subordinated to semiotics.

The Copenhagen School avoided the historical question by sidestepping the distinction between synchrony and diachrony. These terms were avoided in glossematics whereby the structure of a language was reduced to symbols and algebraic laws in order to come to terms with the basically abstract nature of communication. These laws were understood in term of syntagmatics and paradigmatics, formalizations of syntax and paradigm. Once again, there were axes on which language was plotted. Hjelmslev's search for an "algebra of language" focused on accounting for the differences in the forms of the content and its expression. These differences described the play or process of language. Therein lay the crux of structuralism for the Copenhagen School: to reveal the system of language lying behind its process.[42]

A. J. Greimas, who inspired Roland Barthes in Egypt in the early 1940s before becoming the director of general semiotics at the École Pratique des Hautes Études in Paris, continued the work of the Copenhagen School. Assuming semiotics to be a subset of linguistics, as did Hjelmslev, Greimas created what he called the "semiotic square" whereby logic and linguistics were united to provide a taxonomic grid of language for semantic purposes. This square is constructed geometrically with four logical, polar limits in any discussion. Then the logic of the communication is traced by identifying points plotted along diagonals and axes within the square.

It is ingenious and somewhat intimidating to follow the logic of Greimas,[43] who claims to have surpassed the boundaries of both formalism and structuralism by not being limited to either form or structure as viable parameters. His work was grounded in a preference for taxonomy and narrative facts. These characteristics he shared with Leonard Bloomfield, the American whose disciples formed the Yale School to be distinguished from Jakobson, who eventually went to Harvard University where he continued to speak about the need for a structuralist poetics. Bloomfield, however, used a decidedly different tactic than that of Greimas for his version of structuralism. Let us look at Bloomfield's orientation for structure as the basis for his "distributional analysis."

The Yale School   Although conversant with Saussure's *Cours* and the European theorists, Leonard Bloomfield applied a behaviorist approach in linguistics to his classical grammatical training. The American behaviorist tradition had already made its mark in linguistics with Franz Boas (1858–1942), whose studies of Indian languages supported the opinion that languages have their own inner logic, and Edward Sapir (1884–1939), who advanced the theories of linguistic patterns and distributional criteria by which we identify phonemes. Bloomfield observed that the introduction of meaning and intellectual concerns into the study of language vitiated scientific analysis by applying subjective criteria. He thus became an advocate of antimentalism in linguistics and focused on the physical or acoustical properties of language because these phenomena were capable of being measured and investigated objectively. His *Language* (1933) introduced a structural linguistics that would describe all the positions that the elements of a language system could occupy.

Bloomfield's method, called *distributional analysis,* entailed the substitution of the unit under examination with another unit in the same context. If the substitution could be performed without any essential change in the context, then the units being substituted belonged to the same class. These substitutions occurred at the morphological level of language. The morpheme is the smallest language unit having meaning. This distinction implied levels of structure within language because Bloomfield began differentiating language units of a higher or lower rank. Rather than simply using phonemes as basic units of sound, he also defined new terms ending in -*eme* to identify their functions within certain contexts (grammemes, tagmemes, semantemes, etc.). The precision of his terms has led to generations of grammarians who have refined syntactical studies such that the grammatical and semantic structures of a sentence can be appreciated through immediate constituent analysis.

Zellig Harris carried on the Bloomfield method of excluding meaning from the rigor of objective linguistic analysis. His *Methods in Structural Linguistics* (1951) represents the pure form of taxonomic study for which the disciples of Bloomfield are renowned.

During the 1950s, Jakobson arrived at Harvard University and introduced the Prague Circle and the work of the French linguist André Martinet to American linguists. This period saw the Bloomfield method coined as the Yale School because Yale University is where Bloomfield spent the last part of his academic career (1940–47). Meanwhile, Martinet expanded on the theories of the Prague Circle with his insight into the "double articulation" of the phoneme. The phoneme was at the center of two mutually opposing tendencies, one acoustical and the other mental. This confrontation between the American behaviorist approach and the Prague tension between meaning and sound would transform the history of structural linguistics and its influence in the worldwide intellectual community.

Noam Chomsky introduced a theoretical orientation to the behaviorist approach. His theory of a generative or transformational grammar led to prolific explorations of the tensions within language and meaning and to the preference for rationalist rather than empirical method. As early as 1946 Chomsky's mentor, Harris, had published the article "From Morpheme to Utterance" (*Language* 20) and suggested that there was an underlying structure for morphemes. By 1957, Chomsky had developed a grammatical theory clearly distinguishing two levels, the phonological and the syntactical. His *Syntactic Structures* went on to distinguish rules for the transformations between surface and deep structures, competence and performance. He observed that these transformations were dependent on structures whose formal operations were common to many languages in the construction of grammatical sentences.

Chomsky's tendency to create a "universal grammar," as opposed to describing unique laws inherent to individual languages, made his theories very appealing to the French structuralists. Although he rebutted B. F. Skinner's behaviorist method for its lack of sensitivity to the creative impulses in language,[44] Chomsky nevertheless believed in the empirical verification of human intuition and never advocated a "mentalism" that characterized much of French structuralism. Lévi-Strauss, on the other hand, sought to recover a common "human spirit" from the various structures he revealed. This model of the "human spirit," similar to the "innate ideas" of Descartes's rationalism,[45] has the mark of mathematical logic in its tone and its impact on human thinking. And certainly mathematics has played a significant role in the development of French structuralism.

Mathematics and Structure

In 1906, Baudouin de Courtenay pointed out that linguistics could be improved in an alliance with mathematical methods. Since then, the refinement of statistical methods and the theory of probability have provided structural linguistics with wider ranges of development. Jakobson's theories about the binary principles of language have been especially conducive to application in machine translations, information theory, and communication theory.[46] The area of semiotics has developed into a science strongly associated with mathematical formulas whereby languages are analyzed as codes. Such words as encoding, decoding, and transcoding have been invented to speak about the processes used by languages to send information.

The binary principles of languages are especially useful in going from one language to another and from a language to a machine, and in trying to predict messages contained in a given unit of communication. Structural linguistics has shown language to be a system of precisely measurable, finite units. The possibilities of combination among these units are being studied by applying the theory of probability to the units revealed in studies by Troubetzkoy, Bloomfield, Harris, Hjelmslev, Jakobson, and Martinet.

Cybernetics was invented by the American mathematician Norbert Wiener in 1948. The word comes from a Greek etymon meaning "the skill of steering" and applies to the codes in languages and the maps that many French structuralists have theorized and charted about the relationships in languages and from language to other systems of communication (e.g., myths, music, culture, artifacts). Cybernetics has been helpful in elaborating a theory of information, that is, a theory of the invariant structures of language as they relate to the systems of human communication. Algorithms provide formulaic representations of the coding processes relating messages to various languages. The grand assumption is that there are universal laws regularizing all languages. A Russian linguist, Nikolaj Marr (1864–1934), did theorize that four sound combinations (ber, jon, ros, and sol) could account for all the phonetic elements in the languages of the world. This is an ambitious prospectus, similar to the Lévi-Strauss ideal of a universal "human spirit," whereby the differences among human communication systems are ignored for the sake of common denominators.

Lévi-Strauss himself was influenced by the discoveries of mathematical logic. Likewise, Roland Barthes used the vocabulary of coding, decoding, and encoding, especially in the epitome of French structuralist analysis—*S/Z* (1970), an explanation of the short story "Sarasine" by Honoré de Balzac in terms of five narrative codes. The Bourbaki, the pseudonym for a group of French mathematicians, were especially influential for their work in set theory. They conceptualized three systems by which all structures could be understood and related. They spoke of the need for an algebra to represent operations, an order by which to understand relationships, and a topography whereby the concepts of continuity, limitations, and neighborhoods could be mapped. This algebra is an abstract system, reminding us of Hjelmslev's agenda for glossematics, accounting for the laws of the composition of structures and their ensembles.[47]

Mathematics and the sciences provided analogical models for many French structuralists. Set theory influenced Philippe Sollers in 1968 to call his structuralist prospectus for the *Tel Quel* group *Théorie d'ensemble* (Theory of the whole/set theory), with a topography mapped out for a structuralist ideology and theory of writing. Prior to that, during the 1930s, Lévi-Strauss was guided by geology as one of his "mistresses" in his decision to pursue ethnology as a career. The probing of the depths and revealing of the underlying layers of reality appealed to Lévi-Strauss and became one of the trademarks for French structuralism in general. Later, during the 1960s, Michel Foucault would similarly cite a science, archaeology, as the model for the human sciences. All of this leads us to the scientific method as the inspiration for reexamining the social sciences and the humanities. In exploring the stakes of Russian formalism, Bakhtin put his finger on one of the crucial assumptions to be explored by French structuralism in its adaptation of mathematical modeling, "that human consciousness possesses a series of inner genres for seeing and conceptualizing reality."[48] These "inner genres" were thought to be part of a universal spirit unifying human thought.

The death of the humanities occurred concomitantly with this revitalization of the scientific method. The reason for this is the observation common to the French structuralists that human consciousness clouds the true understanding of human nature. This veil of consciousness had to be pulled back. Whereas Louis Althusser noted that "it is impossible to know anything about men except on the absolute precondition that the philosophical (theoretical) myth of man is reduced to ashes,"[49] Lévi-Strauss set an agenda for the human sciences "not to constitute, but to dissolve man."[50] Likewise, Foucault chimed in with: "Rather than the death of God . . . what Nietzsche's thought heralds is the death of his murderer."[51] The effect of all this was to create an intellectual ambiance in which it became important to reveal human thinking in spite of its conscious aims to be human. By 1966, in the midst of the popularity of the French structuralists in Paris, Jean Pouillon attempted to circumscribe the nature of their common practice by noting that their method began with the admission that different ensembles can be related, not despite their differences, but by virtue of the differences being strung together.[52] And mathematical set theory does provide a model for bringing differences together in a common format. But let us return to the differences because therein lie the distinctions made by the French structuralists in adapting the models of their precursors.

The Pursuit of Difference

Although some bystanders have observed French intellectuals rallying to identify with stylish labels such as "formalist," "structuralist," "deconstructionist," and so on, it is curious to note that the French structuralists were quick to differentiate their ideologies from each other. We have already spoken about some of their similarities. Yet their differences are also important because of the debates they engaged in as individuals. These debates demonstrate today the magnetic "critical mass" effect that French structuralism had. It caused many intellectual explosions during that politically volatile period of the 1960s. We will organize our discussion of the mainstream of French structuralism around the five ideologists of the movement and then speak about the intellectual climate they fostered and the fruitful developments of a poststructuralist environment.

The five ideologists were Claude Lévi-Strauss, Roland Barthes, Jacques Lacan, Michel Foucault, and Louis Althusser. In 1980, Maurice Henry drew a cartoon entitled "Le Déjeuner des Structuralistes" (Lunch with the structuralists).[53] It depicted four of these writers sitting in a circle, dressed in primitive garb, listening to Foucault animatedly present an argument. It is significant that the absent one is Althusser. His role was not obvious to Henry, intent on presenting the closed circle of buffoons with Foucault pontificating eagerly, Lacan listening cynically, Lévi-Strauss taking notes earnestly, and Barthes relaxing casually. Althusser is in the wings discussing ideological questions, whose parameters have been constructed on center stage by the four more popular performers.

Each of the five pursued a slightly different and distinguishable course for the impact of structuralism and its eventual demise. Each one was involved in controversies about whether structuralism was an enterprise worth pursuing at the time. I use the word "ideologist" to describe each of them; none of them was really a philosopher. The separate influence each had was not a conscious effort of any of them. Although they all tried to direct when and how they were to be considered "structuralist," the controversies they generated were often beyond their control and continued despite what they wanted to achieve. They all tried to dissociate themselves from the word *structuralist* when the popularity of the expression caused it to be misapplied to their work as a common venture, which it never was.

I will also speak more generally about the intellectual climate fostered by French structuralism. There are three arenas in which significant achievements occurred as spinoffs of the controversies over the structuralist ideologies. These three arenas are politics or its lack thereof (chapter 7), the search for a universal grammar (chapter 8), and the return to the study of first-order narratives (chapter 9). These intellectually fertile spinoffs of French structuralism are being played out to this day.

In what I will discuss as a revival of the humanities, I will conclude with overviews (chapter 10) of how French structuralism still influences major developments in critical thinking, literary theory, and philosophy. In the aftermath of a reputed "death of man," there are resurrections of the human body in identifiable poststructuralist pursuits related to semiotics. All of these developments claim to supersede the limitations of French structuralism. And yet still to be found are remnants of "structure," even if it is called antistructure structure. There is a heritage here, uniquely French in its snobbish appeal and in its political intrigues.

Chapter Two
Lévi-Strauss and the Elusive Human Spirit

Like many of the precursors and the other agents of French structuralism, Claude Lévi-Strauss was not originally French. He was born in Brussels. His grandfather was a rabbi at Versailles. He was educated at the Sorbonne but then went to Brazil to begin his ethnological career. During the early 1940s, he emigrated from France to New York City and began his lifelong association with Roman Jakobson there. His beginnings in every sense were other than French:[1] his birth, his first field experience in ethnology, and his first publication (in Jakobson's journal *Word*) relating structural linguistics and ethnology.[2] During his career, he wrote articles in English and in French. The dual languages of his publications brought with them problems about what he "really" meant and whether he was being translated correctly. His was an identity between cultures, caught in his own otherness. But finally he was accepted within the walls of French culture through his appointment to the Collège de France (1960) and his election to the Académie française (1973).

After being trained in philosophy at the Sorbonne, with Maurice Merleau-Ponty and Simone de Beauvoir as colleagues, Lévi-Strauss began teaching in 1931 and soon became disenchanted. He accepted a visiting appointment in sociology at the University of São Paolo, Brazil, from 1935–39. During this period, he did his only field experience on which to base his whole career as an ethnologist. His notes on the Nambikwara Indians were reconstituted twenty years later in the popular testimony of his trip to Brazil, *Tristes Tropiques* (1955). In fact, this work is not an example of structuralist method. However, the popularity of Claude Lévi-Strauss can be traced back to this work, which he claimed to have begun as a "novel."[3] Whether fact or fiction, *Tristes Tropiques* signaled the beginning of a popular fascination with his exotic writings.

His early career had momentous shifts of background. After his stay in Brazil, he served an uneventful term as a liaison officer in the French army during the "phoney war" until the Occupation and then obtained a position in New York at the New School for Social Science Research. He spent the period 1942–45 writing his study of kinship based on the avuncular (maternal uncle) relationship and other works integrating the structural linguistics learned from his colleague Jakobson into his newly acquired identity as a scientist, that is, as an ethnologist, the French term for social anthropologist. He returned to France in 1947 to be director of the Musée de l'Homme.

After publishing the collaborative study of Baudelaire's poem "Les Chats" in the museum's journal L'Homme, Lévi-Strauss began to distinguish his version of structuralism from that of the Prague structural linguistics. In 1945, he pointed out that traditional linguistics and sociology were in error to focus on terms rather than on the relationships between terms.[4] In the late 1940s and early 1950s, he began to develop a scientific theory to accommodate his vision for a new type of linguistics/sociology/ethnology. The year 1958 was an important one for him. The first volume of *Structural Anthropology* appeared, three years after his *Tristes Tropiques,* and several intellectually influential essays on the nature of "structure" in various social sciences were published. French Structuralism thus began, as Claude Lévi-Strauss was identified as French (because of the place of publication and the language in which these works appeared) and as an advocate of studying "structure," whatever that word meant. Two other events, already mentioned, cemented his acceptance within French culture: his appointment to the Chair of Social Anthropology at the Collège de France in 1960 and his election as one of the forty sanctioned French writers in the Académie française in 1973. It was not a smooth ride along the way, however; he was involved in considerable controversy with formidable scholars. I will present the five most significant debates because they will help us to sort out the contributions and the problems of the Lévi-Strauss strand of French structuralism.

But before proceeding to the controversies, let us look at what the concept *structure* meant for Claude Lévi-Strauss. We have seen that he was involved in qualifying how *form,* as understood by the Russian formalist Vladimir Propp, was distinct from *structure.* For Lévi-Strauss, structure was more comprehensive because it included content, whereas form was defined in contradistinction to content. In addition, structure itself was a grouping of elements related to each other such that any change in one or more elements or relationships modified the remaining elements and/or relationships. When applied to nonliterate cultures in Brazil and in the United States, this view of structure provided Lévi-Strauss with a vision for human thinking. If the structures he discovered were universal and interconnected in common human systems of thinking, structure could have led him to discover the distinctiveness of the "human spirit." This global vision became increasingly abstract, farther from the cultures being studied. It was a grand theory, proposed at a historical moment when political practice was more highly valued. Thus, Lévi-Strauss attracted considerable attention, especially because of the exoticism of his subjects (Amazon and North American Indian tribes) and the schemes by which he analyzed them. To appreciate this controversial view of structure, let us look at how Lévi-Strauss first applied his theories gleaned from structural linguistics to kinship systems.

In Search of "the Atom of Kinship Systems"

British functionalists and American behaviorists studied kinship systems in societies to identify the links between behavior and the verbal attributes of relationships. A case in point was Robert Lowie's *Primitive Society* (1920), which inspired Lévi-Strauss, while in Brazil, to do ethnography. Whereas Lowie's work was empirically based, Lévi-Strauss sought the more universally applicable "elementary structures" of kinship systems.

Similar to Lowie, Lévi-Strauss focused on the avuncular (maternal uncle) relationship. He developed the idea that the avuncular was the key to unlocking the incest taboo. Along the way, he also observed that women are items of economic exchange in society. This latter insight was derived from Marcel Mauss, the first to use the title "social anthropology" at the Collège de France. Mauss's *Essai sur le don* (Essay on the gift) in 1924 viewed gift-giving as links between the members of a given society. The Lévi-Strauss insight about women as items of economic exchange was noted by Simone de Beauvoir and is still praised in contemporary feminist theory.[5]

Despite their favorable reception in feminist circles, his kinship studies were largely overlooked by the anthropological community. The sweeping generalizations about the incest taboo and unilinear kinship relationships went counter to the functionalist, empirically based British and American schools of anthropology. In France, ethnology had not been concerned with kinship systems. Nonetheless, Lévi-Strauss's theories of kinship are important in the development of French structuralism because he applied mathematical reasoning to understand the system underlying relationships. Piaget would point out that kinship systems are examples of algebraic structures[6] and demonstrate that mathematics could be of significant service to the social sciences in search of methodological stability. Lévi-Strauss himself noted that the first geometers and mathematicians were oriented toward humanity rather than toward the physical world.[7] And so it was a natural application of their work to return to the "human sciences," the French appellation for the academic division of the social sciences.

Edmund Leach, a British social anthropologist, took exception to the work of this "chair-borne anthropologist."[8] According to Leach, there were not enough negative examples in the kinship studies. Leach was very uncomfortable with the tendency to universalize examples and ignore empirical data in the pursuit of the "atom of kinship systems." This was the self-declared aim of Lévi-Strauss, to discuss the maternal uncle as the key to understanding kinship relations.[9] But something else happened. The word "myth" was introduced to focus attention on an interest common to both ethnologists and anthropologists.

Mythologizing and Structuralism

In his inaugural lecture upon his appointment to the Social Anthropology Chair at the Collège de France in 1960, Claude Lévi-Strauss gave a timely presentation of the structuralist agenda and parameters. Appropriately translated as *The Scope of Anthropology* (1967), this lecture set up the stakes for distinguishing between the structuralist and the historical "faces" of human reality. These two faces coincide in myths and generate the distinctions between traditional history with its statistical and irreversible sense of time and so-called structural history with its mechanical and reversible sense of time. The latter concept would include mythical language, oral signs, and gestures that are involved in rituals, marriage rules, systems of parenthood, customs, and laws of economic exchange. These concerns would become the domain for anthropology in the area of semiotics not already reserved by linguistics. Myth almost appeared to unite history and anthropology, to represent the two faces of Janus. But Lévi-Strauss went further and stipulated that "our science" would be independent of history: "From now on, history would go it all alone; and society, being outside and above history, could once again assume its normal and crystalline structure, which is not contradictory to humanity as the best preserved of the primitive societies inform us."[10] Of course, this agenda would pique the intelligentsia including the Marxists and the existentialists, the best organized of his opponents.

Meanwhile, the word *myth* became identified with the work of Lévi-Strauss. In general, myth signified a story narrated to explain a culture's origins or weltanschauung. Lévi-Strauss understood myth to be the discourse of a society without any specific speaker.[11] The absence of this speaker allowed him to collect myths and chart them without concern for the narrator, the narratee, or the succession of events in which the story was told. Instead, Lévi-Strauss identified in the stories structures, systems that remained identical despite the obvious differences in the plot due to cultural factors.[12] The myths were analyzed in a state of suspended animation, exemplifying his expectations of structure: the discontinuity between one structure and another and the possibility of tracing a series of transformations from one structure to another.[13] The integrity of each pattern and its relationship(s) to other patterns were capable of being mapped without being challenged by the speaker or the listener of a given myth.

Lévi-Strauss proposed that the ethnologist be a *bricoleur* (a resourceful person) who could assemble the "crystalline structure" of society presented in myths. The translucent, interconnected, and enduring nature of crystals would characterize his program for structure. Meanwhile, the bricoleur was someone who could be ingenious and entrepreneurial enough to discover, beneath the surface, the substantial bedrock of human thinking, this crystalline structure. This bedrock was suggested in the Lévi-Strauss title for one of his anthologies, *La Pensée sauvage* (1963). Sanford Ames reminds us that the words *la pensée sauvage* can mean "untamed thought" or "natural mind."[14] In fact, both meanings are appropriate to describe the insights of myth. On the one hand, human thought, whose parameters are unbridled from those of civilization or history, could well end up untamed if its naked skeleton were exposed. On the other hand, the bricoleur is working with the stuff of the mind in its creatively positive thrust, to portray its values through the stories being narrated in myths. Of course, discovering the pattern of a myth depends on the resourcefulness of the individual. And then one must ask: How imaginative or steadfast is this work in retaining the integrity of culture?

Lévi-Strauss and Jacques Derrida exchanged views on this issue. Derrida characterized the ethnologist as an engineer rather than as a bricoleur.[15] The role of engineer was affiliated more with a technical and architectural enterprise, whereas the bricoleur was more creative in the analysis of myths. Given the scientific claims of Lévi-Strauss for his work, one would expect him to reinforce this claim in 1960 by viewing the anthropologist as an engineer who "conceives and constructs a machine by a series of rational operations."[16] However, after Derrida's observation, Lévi-Strauss vacillated about whether to be the engineer or the bricoleur. His creative impulses as a bricoleur earned him critiques from such major intellectuals as Jean-Paul Sartre, Paul Ricoeur, and Henri Lefebvre. Mary Douglas understood Lévi-Strauss to be an Emmett engineer, that is, an engineer of products with similar imprints due to the same odd pieces in them, because the ethnologist changes the rules in myths while proceeding from one myth to another. She proposed another model for the ethnologist: "For mythic thought a cardplayer could be a better analogy because Emmett can use his bits how he likes whereas the bricolage-type of culture is limited by pattern-restricting rules."[17] Perhaps the cardplayer is a good analogy, provided that the same game is being played by all the players: the rules for tarot do not play out very well if the players are expecting a game of bridge. The problem is how to go from one cultural game to another by interchanging the players.

Translation was at the heart of what Lévi-Strauss did with myths. He often did not know the native languages of the cultures from which the myths originated. Even though he insisted on the distinction between nature and culture to portray myths as uncorrupted by the parameters of civilization or history, he struggled continually with the problem of translating myths from their native culture to his own. Even his own culture was a mixture of Belgian and Jewish beginnings, French language, and American and Brazilian influences. He was haunted by the inexactitudes of translating his own work as well as the myths of other cultures.

The key for avoiding the hex of the translator—*traduttore/traditore* (the translator as traitor)—was to focus on those patterns of the myths where mutual patterns were clearly discernible. This method was an abstract way of avoiding the problem of the incommensurate details that either are not translatable into a given culture or are changed in the process of finding a new context. In addition, Lévi-Strauss pointed out that myths were often transformed from one culture to a neighboring one. This aspect of myth he would call its "nonrecursive" character.[18] This nonrecursive character provides a pattern of transformation, not unlike the "je ne sais quoi" items not translatable into other languages. It is a very slippery practice because Lévi-Strauss found patterns where no one else could before. He even admitted that it was probably inevitable that the analysis of myths entailed a reality "much more homogeneous"[19] than the myths really indicated. Here we have the problem of the treachery to the historical context. His theories about the relationships between history and structuralism would involve him in substantial debates, bringing life to the abstractions resulting from his approach to myths.

What Is Structural History?

The dialectical materialism of Karl Marx was intellectually in vogue in post–World War II France. The leftist intelligentsia were popular as clear alternatives to the Fascist threats of the 1930s and 1940s. Sartre's existentialist agenda contributed to strengthening the role of historical involvement for those disillusioned by war-torn Europe. By 1958, however, "history" was becoming a tired concept in the wake of Stalin and the ideological mudslinging of the cold war. The exotic anecdotes in *Tristes Tropiques* about the ethnologist's work with tribes unacquainted with Western history or civilization were welcome reading for those bored with the promises of historical commitment. The myths of these tribes of Brazil and North America were generally not written. So the *littérature engagée* (committed literature) proposed by Sartre for the postwar generation was not applicable in that these myths were neither literary nor historical.

Lévi-Strauss indicated in the travelogue *Tristes Tropiques* that, in addition to geology (which we already mentioned), Marxism and psychoanalysis were his "mistresses." Psychoanalysis combined with geology to inspire his method of probing surfaces and finding nonconscious scaffoldings for human thinking. Marxism was a more curious "mistress," however. It was a popular position to claim Marxism as his own. Lévi-Strauss even asserted that his notion of "structure" came from Marx.[20] Sartre objected. Lévi-Strauss had not used a dialectical method, according to Sartre, and therefore was not attuned to the historical contexts of myths.[21] The internal history of structures did not constitute "dialectical" history for Sartre. Such a predilection for order leading to the unity of the human spirit would preclude the natural disorders of human events.

Lévi-Strauss responded with a lengthy presentation of his alternative to the historical dialectic, his "totalizing" method. The last chapter of *La Pensée sauvage* is dedicated to replying to Sartre and accusing him of being a "historicist." Lévi-Strauss pointed out that history was only a method and did not correspond to reality. He predicted that the golden era of historical awareness was over and that a new world without human history to form it was evolving. Some onlookers saw this observation as part of an antihumanistic prospectus in French structuralism that continued in the work of Foucault, Althusser, and Lacan. Semiotics, however, now allows us to understand that Lévi-Strauss was separating the conscious overview of history from human thinking and communication in order to portray the integrity of humanity. There was a humanism to Lévi-Strauss in his pursuit of the integrity of the human spirit. His alternative of the "ethnological context" as an exhaustive method for incorporating all the "human sciences" into his analysis of such myths as the Asdiwal myth has earned Lévi-Strauss a following among the respected classical myth scholars at the École Pratique des Hautes Études (see chapter 8). Jean-Pierre Vernant, Marcel Detienne, Pierre Vidal-Naquet, and Nicole Loraux are all actively rethinking classical mythology thanks to Lévi-Strauss and his inspired model for the "ethnological context." However, Sartre did not view Lévi-Strauss as inspired and portrayed him as counterproductive to the Marxist ideals; the "human" sciences were too concerned with Humanity. Instead, Sartre dictated that

Marxism entailed dialectical method to reveal individuals working together in the production of a given historical situation.

This debate portrayed French structuralism as diametrically opposed to historical method as well as to Marxism. And yet Lévi-Strauss had pointed out in 1959 that the methods of the ethnologist and the historian were complementary: the former was concerned with change inside a social group and the latter with change outside the group.[22] But Sartre's rejection of the history of a structure changed the stakes of their disagreement. In response to Sartre's insistence on the historical context for structures, Lévi-Strauss wanted historians to recognize the subordination of history to human thought and its structural laws. Although Lévi-Strauss noted that historians formerly subordinated synchrony to diachrony and that he was calling for a reversal of the correlation, some psychoanalysts understood Lévi-Strauss to be artificially constructing a hierarchical relationship between history and psychological structures.[23] The debate became strident as the French ethnologist referred to the "myth of history" invented by Sartre, "who had a defiant, if not hostile attitude toward science, and who fought all his life to make philosophy a domain hermetically closed to science."[24] Thus, although Lévi-Strauss was the advocate for science on the part of structuralism, Sartre was seen as the philosopher taking up the cause of historicism. This dispute between Sartre and Lévi-Strauss received international attention.[25]

Despite the apparent polarization between history and French structuralism, Lévi-Strauss moderated his position and admitted that even though he did not practice the historical method he reserved it its rights. He reiterated that he never attempted structural analysis without first being enlightened by history. Of course, this was a problem when he studied the myths of illiterate cultures because traditional history could not help. Even when traditional history or philosophy did assist him, the "enlightenment" was a specific adaptation of myth: he understood philosophical and historical contexts to be variants of mythology.[26] What he sought was a way to "totalize" mythmaking, that is, to present the fluidity of its transformations. In 1971, he published an essay called "Le Temps du Mythe" (The time of myth), in which he moderated his view of history in order to include "a mythology which can be causally linked to history in each of its parts" and yet can be appreciated in the integrity of its wholeness.[27] The politics of French structuralism enabled Lévi-Strauss finally to allow for the grid of both history and structure to intersect and thus to affect each other.

From the Outside to the Inside

In his procession toward acceptance within the established French intelligentsia, Claude Lévi-Strauss also developed a political base for French structuralism. Literary journals began to identify him with Barthes, Foucault, Althusser, and Lacan in applying his theories and adopting the structuralist label. At the time, he did not object to being identified with them; it gave him some political support among Paris intellectuals.

Lévi-Strauss also became more involved in political causes. Whereas he pronounced that the structuralist ethnologist primarily wanted to "reduce a multiplicity of expressions to one language,"[28] de Gaulle was elected in 1958 to lead the Fifth French Republic with such determination that Gramont suggested de Gaulle be remembered as "the first structuralist chief of state."[29] Nevertheless, Lévi-Strauss was one of the signers of the "Manifesto of the 121" in 1960 against the Gaullist colonial policies in Algeria. He realized that there was political clout in intellectuals standing together in France. Although some of the present-day French "New Philosophers," like Bernard-Henri Lévy in his *Éloge des intellectuels* (1987), prefer that intellectuals go it alone as touchstones of their integrity, the political climate in France during the 1950s and early 1960s was such that totalitarian control of the nation was ever looming. And France had a long tradition of political involvement by its intellectuals, dating from the clerks of the Middle Ages, to the Enlightenment *philosophes,* to Hugo and Zola in the nineteenth century. In the twentieth century, Julien Benda's *La Trahison des clercs* (The treason of the intellectuals) in 1927 became a manifesto realized by the compassion of André Breton, André Malraux, Raymond Aron, and Sartre, among others. Likewise, humanitarian interests brought together Sartre and Lévi-Strauss in "the Manifesto of the 121" to support Algeria's independence.

Many critics of French structuralism take exception to its antihistorical posture without recognizing the influence of its political inroads. Susan Sontag, for example, understood Lévi-Strauss to have committed to a "moral choice" in not differentiating between primitive and historical types of societies.[30] And indeed the moral choice was one that Voltaire had made in the eighteenth century to combat the infamy of hierarchical distinctions among races. Lévi-Strauss, for his part, wrote a United Nations-sponsored study on racism (*Race et histoire,* Race and history) in 1952, which has been largely ignored in favor of his mythical and structuralist works. This study, however, gave us a humanitarian alternative to xenophobia, the fear of otherness. Therein, Lévi-Strauss proposed a theory of "dynamic tolerance"[31] whereby peoples and their master thinkers look to the future to preclude the barbarism of one culture toward another. Instead of occasional indulgences to excuse present or past behavior of a people by attributing it to the universal character of the group, this tolerance would grow out of the awareness of the one human spirit he claimed to have uncovered in structural thought patterns. For him, as Simon Clarke pointed out, "before the conceptual scheme all that exists is the biological scheme."[32] For example, Lévi-Strauss portrays progress as a procession in leaps and bounds analogically similar to the mutations observed by biologists. In effect, the unity of human biology is duplicated in the realm of human thinking where the discoveries of the structuralists revealed integrity beyond the temporal, geographical, and racial appearances separating cultures.

The integrity of the human spirit claimed by Lévi-Strauss could also be substantiated by the Hermeneutic School of thinkers led by Paul Ricoeur. This group studied the unconscious and traced patterns in human thinking, especially in the Bible and other ideologically influenced texts. However, Ricoeur objected to the Lévi-Strauss prospectus because the ethnographer did not reveal information that led to a better understanding of the self. Lévi-Strauss noted, in reply, that we are all "prisoners of our subjectivity" because we cannot comprehend anything from both the inside and the outside at the same time.[33] This was a political statement by Lévi-Strauss because he was stating his preference for a humanitarian ideal rather than for a predilection for self-centered ethnology with its ensuing hierarchical judgments of a culture. Lévi-Strauss would not give himself the identity of a master thinker despite his innovative role in French structuralism. Looking back in 1980 upon his accomplishments, he preferred to see himself as an "artisan" working with certain specific cultures to uncover patterns and similarities. And yet the politics of his time would not let him forget that he did have a major impact on how others understood the relationships of myths and culture.

The Demythologizing of Culture

The interaction suggested by Lévi-Strauss between structure and history was inspired by his vision of a System possessing cohesion and equilibrium and pointing to the stability of the human spirit. The System was a grand scheme that earned Lévi-Strauss the wrath of traditional Marxists such as Henri Lefebvre, who could also see that this controversy opened up the possibility for a new humanism and for its redefined role relative to dialectical thinking.[34] The "totalizing" approach preferred by Lévi-Strauss over the dialectical method encompassed a network of myths within a society pointing to an ensemble beyond the boundaries of the cultural identity of the given society. Ricoeur called this ensemble neo-Kantian without a transcendental subject in that Lévi-Strauss was idealistic about the "human spirit" before verifying its existence. Lévi-Strauss agreed that "the concept of structure is not amenable to an inductive definition."[35]

Instead, the nonconscious cohesive power of a structure demonstrates the deductive effect of human thinking on how cultures become identifiable. The grouping of certain characteristics around a common pattern exemplifies the organizational and determining power of the human mind on cultural formation. Lévi-Strauss's declared purpose was to reveal the assimilating effect of the "myth of monoculture" on society.[36] The hierarchical domination of a single culture (male, Western, Caucasian, etc.) evaluating another culture imposes strictures on how the other culture is perceived. According to Lévi-Strauss, the principle of cultural differentiation has been overutilized and can be corrected by noting the same human spirit present in all cultures.

The structures identified by Lévi-Strauss from geographically and historically disparate cultures are often based on polarized values, some similar to and others different from each other. The effect is to show that human thinking does have common organizational patterns despite such apparent differences as time, place, race, or gender. His early comment on the way a tribe organizes its space is revealing: "The structure of the village does something more than make possible the refined working of the institution; it both sums up and insures the relationships between man and the universe, society and the supernatural world, and between the living and the dead."[37] Thus, the network of meanings connecting humanity to its world is reflected in the ways in which daily life is organized and narrated. "Narrated" is crucial because stories entail not only the semiotic setting but also the larger cultural setting or system in which the communication took place.[38]

Although Lévi-Strauss insisted that he was not a philosopher of structuralism, he noted, in his acceptance speech to the Collège de France, that ethnology distinguished itself from sociology because of the more clearly philosophical ethnological method. What he meant is that the attitude of his type of ethnology is more clearly defined: he wanted ethnology to discover that ideal of the human spirit. However, Ricoeur's hermeneutic mind could not accept Lévi-Strauss as having discovered this ideal. From Ricoeur's point of view (the impact of symbolism on human thinking), the linguistic method of Lévi-Strauss was a severe problem because it tended to empty the content of an expression and ignore meaning in order to speak about arrangement and order.[39] Thus, the binary tensions observed by Lévi-Strauss were oversimplified because they occurred only on the plane of the form, to return to

Hjelmslev's linguistic distinction between form and content, applicable to an ethnological analysis of culture. It is ironic to see simplicity in the intricate diagrams of his structures. Nevertheless, as Lévi-Strauss himself remarked about previous scholars of myths, he too may be subject to the same judgment as a purveyor of yet another myth of the human spirit: "One of the great difficulties in myth analysis, or at least in writing books on myths, comes from the fact that the author inevitably leaves his or her mark on the synthesis being made and thereby creates a reality much more homogeneous than are the myths themselves."[40]

Lévi-Strauss was the first of the major ideologists of French structuralism. His theories influenced the four other major ideologists to take slightly different courses under the banner of the structuralist name. And yet some of those who were most affected by him claimed that Lévi-Strauss was not essentially structuralist.[41] This may be true. But posterity will remember him primarily for having taken the first courageous steps with his theories about the distinctiveness of the structuralist perspective. The negative humanism of his prospectus for structuralism directly affected Foucault, Althusser, and Lacan. The echoes of Lévi-Strauss reverberated throughout the francophone world after he pronounced that "I believe the ultimate goal of the human sciences to be not to constitute, but to dissolve man."[42]

Meanwhile, in the literary domain, Roland Barthes did constitute a "new humanism" by revealing the stakes in the myths of French culture while also dissolving the author as conscious creator of a cultural artifact. Barthes expanded on the Lévi-Strauss presentation of myths to search for an aesthetic of writing and reading in the modern world. The theories entailed by his search galvanized a whole generation of writers to provide alternatives to the Sartrean existentialist model for engaged writing.

Chapter Three
Barthes and Reading Obliquely

Roland Barthes seemed destined not to be a university professor. After being plagued by recurring bouts of tuberculosis with extended periods in sanatoriums, he did not finish the required terminal degree of the doctorat d'état in the French university system. But Susan Sontag correctly characterized him as "one of the great modern refusers of history."[1] Despite the odds against him, he succeeded in becoming a French university professor by entering through the "back door": the École Pratique des Hautes Études from 1961 to 1977, when he finally earned a chair in the prestigious Collège de France. On the strength of the popularity of his publications, beginning with his first article on Plato's *Crito* in 1933, and his fame as the incarnation of the structuralist "new criticism," he was able to select the name "literary semiotics" for his chair at the Collège de France. By 1977, Lévi-Strauss and Foucault had already become faculty members there; the addition of Barthes represented the complete intellectual domination of the Collège de France by the ideologists of French structuralism.

During the 1940s, Roland Barthes was no structuralist. Like Lévi-Strauss, for a time he was an outsider in French intellectual circles. Always the teacher, Barthes had held positions at Bucharest in 1948 and at Alexandria in 1949. In this latter appointment, he learned about structural linguistics from A. J. Greimas, a specialist in semantics. During this period, Barthes was struggling for a sense of writing at an oblique stance from Sartre's "committed literature."[2] The word "writing" (*écriture*) was not diametrically opposed to the "literature" advocated in 1948 by Sartre (*Qu'est-ce que la littérature?*, "What's literature?), in which the writer had a clearly defined ideological role in communicating with society. Barthes, however, was promoting writing with a life of its own, floating free of historical association with its writer's designs. But, existentialism was in full bloom. Aware that only one out of every two French persons was reading anything at all, Barthes realized that his own readers were few indeed.[3]

From 1947 to 1950, Barthes published a series of articles in *Combat,* elaborating Sartre's understanding of Albert Camus's *écriture blanche* as demonstrated in the novel *L'Étranger* (1942). Camus's narrator spoke about rather

33

than exemplified the absence of connections between the subject and the world. Barthes elaborated that this was the condition of modern writing, but he would have to wait until the novels of Alain Robbe-Grillet (b. 1922) in the early 1950s to see the fulfillment of this prophecy. Barthes would be one of the first to explain to the world the appropriate visions represented in the Robbe-Grillet writings. Meanwhile, Barthes theorized that modern writing was transcending history and collected these theories in an anthology published in 1953 as *Le Degré zéro de l'écriture*. These theories were prophetic rather than synchronized with the writing practices of the time.

Between 1954 and 1956, Barthes continued to exemplify a journalistic passion with contributions of the "mythology of the month" to *Les Nouvelles littéraires*. These mythologies, not to be confused with the myths discovered by Lévi-Strauss, were cultural manias narrated by Barthes to expose the way in which meaning was invented in the daily activities of life in France. That is, the French believed in the importance of certain components of their daily lives. Barthes provided narratives called "mythologies" about the meaning of such heterogeneous items as wrestling, advertising, plastic, soap bubbles, striptease, and the Tour de France, among other apparently naive components of daily survival. Often, he would expose French cultural obsessions such as a belief in the goodness of wine. Although these reflections do not have, overall, theoretical cohesion, one essay—"Le Mythe Aujourd'hui" (Myth today)—does point out that the structures of myth are manifest, as opposed to the Lévi-Strauss analyses whereby latent meanings are exposed. For Barthes, understanding myths is merely a question of the angle from which one looks at them. These myths were analyzed by Barthes from his oblique angle in journalistic fragments and then collected in book form as *Mythologies* in 1957.

As we reread these early Barthes writings today, we can see his concern with how signs signify and how cultures arbitrarily assign meanings to recurring phenomena. He had a vision of the system of "myths" whereby the "desires" of French culture were represented in the narrative of its myths. In 1958, French structuralism began to take shape with Lévi-Strauss, and Barthes was dovetailing the linguistic lessons learned from Greimas, Benveniste, and others into a similar mode. Barthes then realized his own personal vision and moved through his association with structural linguistics in five separate stages: (1) explaining the differences caused by the oblique angles from which he looked at myths; (2) viewing grammar as a paradigm for all narratives; (3) presenting semiology as part of a larger model in language; (4) understanding game-playing as a crucial insight into the practice of writing; and (5) portraying desire as the basic component of signification and the key to appreciating the relationship of language to his own physical presence as a writer. These stages help us to understand his move from metalanguage and science during the period 1966 to 1970 by presenting these concerns as a part of his intellectual evolution in dealing with the nonconscious.

Barthes thus exemplified a new humanism as structural linguistics enabled him to observe words from an oblique angle and to see the structures of symbols. His ability to view language obliquely makes him a transitional figure, between the symbolic myths of Lévi-Strauss and the imaginary unconscious of Lacan. Lévi-Strauss yearned for the abstract human spirit contained in myths. Now that we understand the unfulfilled symbolic dream of Lévi-Strauss, Barthes represents a stark contrast in French structuralism, as he left us with real alternatives in the writer's body, looking askance at the physical presence of the words from his own writings. His look was an unconscious participation in the imaginary, a psychoanalytic concept developed by Lacan as the triangular link between the symbolic and the real, as I shall elaborate in chapter 4. Meanwhile, Barthes's models for reading have become signposts on the road through what he called the "heroic period of structuralism."[4]

Focusing on Differences Rather than Repetition

Just as Lévi-Strauss was becoming popular with his anthropological models of structuralism, Barthes became well-known as the advocate of the new French literary criticism. Opposing the "university criticism" of the French literary establishment, he sought to "complicate" history by introducing a "historical pluralism."[5] In the February 1963 issue of *Les Lettres Nouvelles,* he began a presentation of the "anthropology of the Racinian man," which eventually resulted in the publication of the pamphlet *Sur Racine* later that same year. Raymond Picard (b. 1917), a professor of French classicism at the Sorbonne, answered Barthes by accusing him of being impressionistic, relativistic, pseudoscientific, and sexually cynical about Racine's characters. This reply, published in *Le Monde* in 1964, was expanded in 1965 into another pamphlet called *Nouvelle Critique ou nouvelle imposture?*

But Barthes was providing an alternative voice to the tired and banal pronouncements collectively labeled "university criticism." He replied with a proposal for a "science of literature," apparently modeled on the terms, theories, and methods of structural linguistics in his *Critique et vérité* (1966). Thus, a structuralist battle of the books began. Like Lévi-Strauss, Barthes was an outsider in the university establishment and was hurling his own Molotov cocktail into the den of the comfortable professors doing literary history in the style of Gustave Lanson,[6] that is, an evolutionary model whereby the biography of an author provided the motives for writing and insights into the "objective" recovery of the meaning of literature. As Barthes pointed out, this method was arrogantly positivistic and self-assured: "When the Author has been found, the text is 'explained'—victory to the critic."[7] But it was a Pyrrhic victory in that the text slipped away, having a life of its own. Aware of the cleavage between writer and writing, Barthes chose to respect this lacuna and promoted a model of "structuralist activity," shifting the focus to the text after proclaiming the Death of the Author.

Barthes developed a model that could be called the ideology of the readerly text. Although he coined the expression of a readerly text in 1973 in *Le Plaisir du texte* (*The Pleasure of the Text*), he was unconsciously moving toward this concept with his early theories of writing, myth, and interpretive criticism (versus academic or university criticism). Whereas "university criticism" perpetuated empty bourgeois models of the hierarchies, Barthes stressed the example of myth analysis, which teaches us that "myth hides nothing."[8] There is no hidden meaning to be derived from the psyche of the author or originator.

Barthes gave us the model for a readerly text in *S/Z* (1970). This is a transitional work pointing beyond structuralism toward semiotics. And it is also the apogee of French structuralist literary analysis. Although Culler does not see a model offered by Barthes,[9] Sontag does correctly identify the modern aesthetic interests of Barthes and points to his insight that the surface is as informative as the depth of a message.[10] The aesthetic on which *S/Z* is constructed attributes the text to a web-like narrative structure. In a sample of this narrative structure, Barthes developed five separate themes which he called codes, and which had formed the basis for a short story by Balzac called "Sarrasine." His analysis proceeded according to 516 fragments or lexias whereby the web was exposed in all its intricate networking of the five codes. Some critics understand *S/Z* as an antistructuralist work written as an ironic statement about the scientific pretensions of French structuralism; *S/Z* exhausts the short story "Sarrasine" so that the original narrative is lost in the analysis. But Barthes would have description be understood as a shifting in structure.[11] Unlike those in academic criticism who claimed objectivity, he acknowledged that another discourse was inevitable as he read and constructed meanings.

The "other" discourse was the cleavage of the History advanced by traditional literary historians and the anecdote or story. Barthes played with the double meaning in the French word *histoire* (history and story).[12] He inserted a wedge between the two and insisted that the bar separating the two meanings could only be traversed once, similar to the bar signifying the relationships of the two characters Sarrasine and Zambinella in the title *S/Z*. Thus, Barthes refused to accept literary hierarchies established "canonically" by literary historians. He implemented the Saussurian linguistic arguments, about the arbitrariness of meaning and the irretrievable signifier to a literary context, and achieved an aesthetic of difference. He was not as mercurial as he would appear to be at first glance. Instead, he was shifting his perspectives as he explored answers to the question "What is the place of reality in the structure of discourse?"[13] The various oblique angles of his perspectives on myths and his new appreciation of writing were all part of an aesthetic of difference. This aesthetic has been developed in the works of Gérard Genette, Gilles Deleuze, Michel Serres, Tzvetan Todorov, and Julia Kristeva. In fact, *ideology* is a better term than *aesthetic* in speaking about Barthes's work, because others gave specific form to the framework of ideas he had sketched. Barthes outlines an ideology of reading whereby the plurality of perspectives and meanings are privileged. The parameters of this ideology were identified in his research into the syntagms and paradigms of narratives.

Structure as Grammar

Buoyed by the popularity of his debate with Picard, Barthes rallied other theorists outside the established French university community into a collaborative elaboration of a "science of literature." In 1966, he organized essays by Umberto Eco, Tzvetan Todorov, Gérard Genette, Claude Bremond, and Christian Metz in a now classic issue of the journal for the École des Hautes Études, *Communications*. His lead article in that issue, "Introduction à L'Analyse Structurale des Récits" ("Introduction to the Structural Analysis of Narratives," translated in *A Barthes Reader*), gives an overview of the issues for the development of narratology, a study of narrative suggested by his proposal for a science of literature. The other contributors to that issue— along with Gerald Prince, Teun van Dijk, and A. J. Greimas—have pursued this study of narrative such that narratology (see chapter 8) has now become an international venture.

Barthes asked the question in that article about which "grammar" regulates the syntagmatic chain of narratives. The word *syntagmatic* was borrowed from Roman Jakobson and his poetic grid of paradigmatic and syntagmatic axes. Whereas the paradigmatic axis entails paradigms of the symbolic functioning of languages from one level of abstraction to another, the syntagmatic axis is the contextual meaning language derives from the horizontal juxtaposition of words next to each other. Hence, the syntagmatic chain of a narrative refers to the internal context of a story's elements, that is, its characters, events, actions, and so on. The analogy between the structure of language and that of narrative was the next step after Lévi-Strauss had shown that structural linguistics could be helpful in identifying hidden patterns in myths. The examples of Troubetzkoy, Hjelmslev, and Greimas (see chapter 8) were heuristic for Barthes, in that their work could be applied to narratives and thereby give literary criticism a scientific status, especially in the wake of machine translations and cybernetic languages.

Barthes's vision for the grammatical model of narrative was linked to an idealistic dream from the medieval curriculum of the trivium. The trivium had brought together grammar, rhetoric, and dialectics as disciplines containing the secrets of language. Barthes became engaged in exploring how structural linguistics could expose these very secrets for modern writing. Disenchanted by the empirical claims for literary history in the French traditions of Lanson ("a dream of scientism"[14]), he saw instead the paradigm offered by the linguistic concern for the grammaticality of sentences: a homology for narrative structure. The word *homology* meant a paradigm linking one structure to another. Through his brilliant use of neologisms he thus linked the medieval trivium with contemporary writing practices. He often used Greek or Latin etymons to describe contemporary narratives. For example, he presented the writers Sade, Fourier, and Loyola as *logothètes,* creative transformers of language.[15]

The neologism *logothètes* reinforced the grammatical distinction between active and passive voice applied by Barthes to the vocations of writers (*écrivains* and *écrivants*). The *écrivain* realized the intransitivity of the writing task, whereas the *écrivant* (a neologism invented from the present participle of the verb "to write") consciously and creatively manipulated language to achieve a desired result. Although the passive voice is appropriate to the modern condition of writing ("deprived of all transitivity, forever doomed to signify itself at the moment when it wants to signify only the world"[16]), whereby the writer is written by writing, many writers believe they are/were in control of writing and can communicate themselves to their readers. This tension between the active and passive voices of writers was well conceived by Barthes in a lecture entitled "To Write: An Intransitive Verb?"[17] given at a Johns Hopkins Seminar on the French structuralists in 1966. In this talk, he used the term *middle voice,* borrowed from linguistic studies on Greek and other languages by Meillet and Benveniste, to describe the modern literary sense of writing. The middle voice is a verb quality whereby the grammatical subject is affected by the verbal action. The middle voice obligates the subject to remain inside the action. (For example, in the sentence "I sacrifice myself,"

"I" is affected by the action of doing the sacrifice.) Barthes proposed in this lecture to assign the middle voice to the verb "to write" as an explanation of the complex voice relating the writer and writing. In another essay, he called Voltaire the "last happy writer" because of the "felicity" of that writer whose reader was listening to his voice. But that condition no longer exists. Instead, the writer's voice is lost in the syntagmatic chain of language.

Another grammatical predicament homologous to the narrative is the problem of inflection and conjugation. Just as grammar regulates the endings, tenses, voices, positions of words—and the gender in French— according to their context in a sentence, so a narrative becomes increasingly deterministic as the context is more complexly developed. The choices are determined by the context-sensitive language. Barthes identified myth as an inflection[18] to describe the variations of a plot that the same narrative undergoes in different cultural, historical, and geographical settings. As he examined the syntagmatic chain of narrative in more detail, however, he encountered the intersection of grammar and rhetoric in narrative "inflections." For example, he discovered four classes (functions, indices, parametrical relations, and informants) of narrative units, basically identifiable along horizontal and vertical axes, the two identified by Jakobson as syntagmatic and paradigmatic, reflecting the functioning of metaphor and metonymy.

The problem with the two axes is that they refer to two meanings in tension, the paradigmatic and the syntagmatic chains. The paradigmatic (vertical, metonymic) axis takes the analysis of narrative outside the story so that the internal (i.e., grammatical) rules cannot regulate the description of a story. The neologisms used by Barthes were a reflection of his own inability to stay within the limitations of grammar. These plays on words thereby implemented a paradigmatic relationship between his readings and language, between his body and the physicality of words. For example, because *saveur* and *savoir* have the same etymology,[19] his argument in *Le Plaisir du texte* for the eroticism of reading had a dynamics internal to the nature of language. The nature of language was not necessarily literary, however, so that as he moved increasingly into the area of rhetoric, he realized that his domain was truly that of semiology, the science of signs also known as semiotics.

Decoding the *Homo Significans*

Ferdinand de Saussure was the first to relate language to semiology. He pointed out that linguistics was a subset of the larger study of signs, which he called semiology. Barthes inverted the relationship by making semiology a subdiscipline of linguistics. Effectively, language was thus a model for all sign systems, according to Barthes. Because of his association with the word *semiology* and his Chair in Literary Semiology at the Collège de France, Barthes is often considered to be the founder of semiology. Although there are some who insist that semiotics and semiology refer to the same study of signs, it was clear that Barthes gave priority to language as the basis for *semiology,* a term he used throughout his writing career.

Barthes focused on the sign as a crucial component of the ideological relationship among writer, writing, and reader. In a brilliant analysis of Barthes, Ungar has reminded us that "ultimately, there is no escape from the dominance of signs because meaning is projected out of a need to assume mastery and appropriate difference."[20] In this vein, Barthes described humanity as the species *homo significans,* since his studies of rhetoric revealed the human tendency to encode messages in signs of different sorts. The distinction between message and code was crucial to his semiological mission. The paradigms within narratives revealed symbolic functioning to be inherent to storytelling and to the human need to communicate. Rhetorical analysis sensitized him to how rhetoric itself is a code and requires a methodological attitude[21] to decipher its ideological weaving of language, society, and history. The syntagmatic chain in the message pointed him toward rhetoric and the paradigms whereby he understood the semiological functioning of *homo significans.*

Barthes studied Japanese culture for its commentary on the unique internal cohesion of Western sign systems and on the universality of the process of symbolization. The juxtaposition of Eastern and Western sign systems highlighted the deficiencies of sign systems not allied with ideological ties to society, history, or geography. One major discovery in Japan was that there is nothing beneath the surface of sign systems: what you see is what you get. Barthes had observed a similar phenomenon with myths. It was not a question of probing the surface to try and reveal a deep structure of the unconscious or another level of subliminal activity. Rather, it was a question of oblique angles, of perspective. The Westerner looks at the haiku, a Japanese lyrical poem, and thinks it empty of meaning because of the density of the Japanese ideograms to readers of the Roman alphabet. And yet the haiku is pregnant with meaning for the informed Japanese reader. Likewise, as an outsider to the Bunraku puppet theater, Barthes still decoded it.

We are struck by Barthes's recurring anxiety, with respect to all language but generated by his displacement in the Japanese culture, about "an unarticulated fear that language itself means nothing, that it is merely an automaton's gesture flagging down the void."[22] He had concerns about forgeries, counterfeit signs, and inauthentic writing. His *Roland Barthes par Roland Barthes* (1975) manifests these intuitions that there is perhaps nothing at the center of the sign. The arbitrary character of the sign points to the absence of the signified. The onion became the exemplary analogy for the structure of the sign because the successive folds lead to nothing at the center, a naked absence. Neither the writer, nor the reader, grasps any prior reality in writing. So what difference does a writer make? According to Philip Thody, the difference made by Barthes is as a writer "who believes that the only way to change society is to change the language in which people think . . . [and] to write in a highly original manner and to annoy people by so doing."[23] Indeed, Barthes's word play continued throughout his writings. But rather than the word, the play was finally more important. The medieval trivium did complement grammar and rhetoric with dialectics.

Larvatus Prodeo

Barthes's favorite maxim was *Larvatus prodeo*: "I advance pointing to my mask." Structuralism allowed him to pose from the various oblique angles of his perspectives. Henri Lefebvre took exception to this structuralist rubric by pointing out that each writer was using "structure" to mean something different; the consequence was that structuralism was leading its readers toward obfuscation.[24] But the very nature of "structure" promoted this masking of meaning, because the relationship imbued by the overarching ties could be viewed from the differing elements in the ensemble. In his essay "Structuralist Activity," Barthes noted that there were two distinct operations involved in this enterprise: (1) dividing the work into parts (*découpage*, a word taken from the film industry meaning to organize a narrative into scenes or frames), and (2) bringing the parts together (*agencement*, a word clearly implying the active ordering by an agent). In this latter operation, Barthes saw himself in control. The masks were those of a clown engaged and engaging the spectators in the playfulness of language. Rather than the obfuscation pointed out by Lefebvre or a profundity sought by Lévi-Strauss in going beyond the mask of appearances, the mask for Barthes was part of the playfulness of the sign, arbitrary in its motivation and also in its ties between the signifier and signified. Meaning became for him a slippery venture, in which he became increasingly unsure of his footing.

The third component of the trivium, dialectics, came into the Barthes prospectus as he began to understand the ludic dimensions of the sign. The semiological dialectic involved, for Barthes, the relationships of signs to their originators and recipients. Signs could not simply be retrieved in their objective meaning. Barthes realized that signs were composed and received in specific dialectical bonds. Just as his writings still defy synopsis by virtue of their fragmentation and shifts in focus, so his contribution to French structuralism provides his example of literature as the "readerly" practice of an ongoing, irretrievable play of words.[25] Within this play controlled or at least implemented by writers like him, the author has no life beyond the name associated with the writing ("Writing is the destruction of every voice, of every point of origin"[26]). The beginning of the existence of writing entails the death of its author in back of the mask. The reader sees the mask of the writing, but never the face of the author. Meanwhile, the writer is affected by the writing because the life of the writing gives the writer his or her identity by the association of the writing with the writer's name. Barthes adopted this view from Gide and Michelet who understood their writings in this way.[27]

Barthes's interests in typography, calligraphy (e.g., his analyses of Erté's fascination with the alphabet and women's bodies; photographs of Barthes's handwriting in *Roland Barthes par Roland Barthes*), and the grain of the voice ensued from his concern with the life of writing in the middle voice. The middle voice in grammar can be developed in dialectics to speak about the concomitant death of the author and the life of the writing and its reader in the grammatically copulative verb. Of course, the copula also suggests sexual activity and links the playfulness of language to the desire of the reader, a physicality strongly emphasized by Barthes. Erté, who experimented with sketches of women's bodies variously contorted to imitate letters of the alphabet, provided Barthes with a literal model of the juxtaposition of writers' and readers' bodies to the physicality of writings. He ignored the feminist issues at stake in Erté's drawings and claimed that Erté's art resided in the embodiment of letters in human form.[28]

Likewise, Barthes's essay "The Grain of the Voice" (the title was also used for a collection of his essays published in 1981 in Paris) reaffirmed his interest in the modern concern with the enduring quality of the sign. The "granular" quality of the voice, its timbre, is the feature in a singer's or speaker's voice identified with that individual without reference to any other past name or tag. Here again we have the intersection of the performance of a sign with the recipient in a manner unbeknownst to the sender, because, internally, sounds we produce are not understood as others hear them. Barthes used a similar perception of atonal music to speak about the reading of modern texts, such as Philippe Sollers's novel *H* (1973), in which an atonal structure of themes, ideas, and anecdotes gives the reader an opportunity to shift from one to the other without having to remember the unity of tone.[29] Derrida would later develop this aspect of the spoken voice as exemplary of the sign's self-referentiality. Within French structuralism, the seeds were thus being sown for its own demise in deconstructionism.

Barthes's choice to analyze Erté reflected an increasing tendency on his part to prefer the anagrammatic to the linguistic theories of Saussure. The anagrammatic side of Saussurian influence encouraged explorations into the paradigms of language rather than the descriptions of language practiced by the followers of Bloomfield in the American School of structuralism. The analogy of interpreting signs to reading music was a fruitful one used by Barthes throughout his writings. For example, he spoke of the importance of reading Beethoven thus: "You have to position yourself to this music so that you are, or even better you are acting as, a performer who knows how to displace, cluster, combine, and arrange; this 'structuring,' possibly an overly used expression, is very different from constructing or reconstructing, in the classical sense."[30] Structuring thus became allied, in the later part of Barthes's career, with playfulness, the paradigms of meaning Jakobson had once ascribed to the vertical axis in the grid of signification. As guided by the writings of Barthes, paradigms would become universal features of all semiological systems.

The masks of Roland Barthes became ever more striking in this playful phase of his writing when he explored the dialectical component of the medieval trivium. He was a clown of sorts, using masks and mirrors to entertain while displaying the joy of the mind at play. Many spectators (e.g., *TLS,* 12 October 1967; the *New Yorker,* 22 September 1980) saw the mandarin clown at work in Barthes trying to set the style from his Olympian perspective. Of course, this observation depends on the assumption that Barthes could maintain that single, condescending voice from on high. But actually he spoke from different voices and insisted on shifting his perspectives. The tone of his voice changed from that of teacher to that of wondering schoolboy demonstrating to us the joys of reading and the structure as a bond between the text and its reader. In 1978, some of his students put together a parody of his "styles" in *Le Roland Barthes sans peine* (The painless Roland Barthes) and provided yet another paradigm of his playfulness. When he saw this parody, he became very sad. He had a glimpse that all his writings were being mistakenly thought to lack "high seriousness." And there was the rub. This reader had been misread because his ludic aesthetics had been literally applied to his own readings.

The Ultimate Irony of Desire

French structuralism teaches us that lack of control is the inevitable fate of those who use language, despite their conscious aims. Language is presented as governing human thinking and the ways in which we express and give meaning to our thoughts. Within his writing career, however, Barthes taught us that writing contains the seeds for the self-destruction of structure itself. The literary fragments in Barthes's writings, the arbitrary alphabetical or numerical ordering of his reflections, and his scientific pretensions in adapting the concepts of structural linguistics to a semiological vision all represent his struggle with the roles of writer and reader controlling or being controlled by language. This struggle is the activity of desire within a reader. All who struggle with signs are readers because they must interpret either their own signs or those of others and thereby shift from one code to another. Barthes observed that reading is "desiring the work,"[31] that is, wanting to be one with the text being read. This desire, whose purest form he identifies as a pastiche, is at the core of all signification.

Frustrated by the published parody of his playful styles, Barthes was about to leave the Collège de France in February 1980, when he was struck by a laundry truck. Less than a month later, he died. And yet his works continue to appear. Beyond his death, we have seen, between 1980 and 1989, the publication of eight volumes of his essays and reflections. And there will probably be more "discoveries" and/or forgeries. So the initials RB signing his writings perpetuate a life for Roland Barthes beyond his own physical death, that is, beyond the death of his desires for his writings. Ironically, in his absence, his writings become his death masks and achieve the maximum impact from their presence. The reason for this is that the writings have a desire of their own. Appropriately, Barthes the reader noted in his *Le Plaisir du texte* that "the text you write must prove to me that it desires me."[32] This is a realization of his earlier insight concerning the death of the author that a text's unity was to be found in its destination rather than in its origin. The sign is thus fulfilled prophetically. It looks forward rather than backward and projects its own desire for self-realization in the reader's determination of meaning.

In a volume of essays called *Incidents* (1987), selections from his journal in 1979 indicate that he was also frustrated by not being able to write continuously. The flow of expression from his readerly role to his writerly role was interrupted and fragmented. He was reading signs all around him and wanted to express his insights about them. But some sort of "writer's block" became a paradigm for the bar that separated the signifier from the signified, the referent from the sign. Just as one could not go back to recover the origins of the signifier or the sign, so he could not reproduce his readerly activity. He was not able to peer behind his own mask to see his face in all its nakedness. Instead, his was the look of Orpheus.

When Barthes's mother died in 1978, his loss reverberated throughout his writings. In *La Chambre claire* (1980), he sadly recalled trying to find his mother in the Winter Garden when he was five years old. The idea reminds us of the picture in *Roland Barthes par Roland Barthes* of his mother holding him in her arms at about the same age. The absence of his mother set a sad tone that dominated his writings and conformed to the paradigm of forfeiture (the referent, the signified) associated with the condition of language. This tone recalled his fascination with the mythological tale of Orpheus and Eurydice whereby Orpheus destroyed Eurydice by looking back at her after rescuing her from Hades. The look backward, a conceit for what history encourages us to do, destroys the integrity of that event and composes another event melding the present *homo significans* who is looking, listening, and reading with the object being received. Once we look backward, the event in back of us is forever transformed into something else tinged with memory and the present fixation of that event in contemporaneous terms. The simulacrum, the trace of reality, was an important concept for Barthes, later to be developed by Jean Baudrillard (b. 1929). Basically, Barthes expressed angst at never closing the gap between what he wanted to say and what was said. The sadness about having destroyed Eurydice, even after being forewarned by his own theories about the nature of writing and semiology, would forever loom over Barthes's reflections. His desire was inevitably thwarted because, in later life, it was often unrequited, as one homosexual experience (17 September 1979) sadly testifies: "I saw evidence that I would have to abandon boys because there was no desire on their part for me, and because I am either too scrupulous or too awkward to impose my desire."[33] He thus admitted his own powerlessness with desire.

As Orpheus, Barthes was also a musician who could sing songs of unrequited love to his Eurydice, the reader reciting paeans about readings. This Eurydice was embodied in his writings, which, like her, were outside his control once he decided to look upon them and thus transform them into the object of his desire. Writing seduced him and then forever held him at bay by slipping away from his desires. The coquettish nature of writing frustrated Barthes the writer and yet was also responsible for the birth of the reader. Writing and signs concomitantly give birth to Orpheus while consigning Eurydice to death. Barthes was caught up in the bar that separated Orpheus/ Eurydice, the loss of self felt from one to the other.

The transition from one to the other was a difficult passage for Barthes. The ending and the beginning of relationships were trying times; he was not certain what space he occupied. In his autobiographical *Roland Barthes par Roland Barthes,* he referred to himself as I, him, you, and me. These multiple voices of the self were developments of the oblique angles of his readerly ideology. Some have thought him too mercurial in moving from one stance to another. But his sensual appreciation of the granular voice and the physicality of Erté's alphabet led his changing perspectives toward a sense of intellectual grounding.[34] *Le Plaisir du texte* (1973) had already noted his awareness that "my body does not have the same ideas I do."[35] He had been intrigued by the historian Jules Michelet's study of physical relics[36] prior to writing the history of a period. The symbiotic union always attracted Barthes. Michelet's connections with people historically, the copulative nature of the verb, the dialectic of reader and text, the rapport between teacher and student, the transfer between analyst and analysand were all variations of a much larger concern for the grounding of his being in others. Ungar's insight is pertinent: "Barthes's book of love is then very much also a book of the body."[37]

The culinary pleasures Barthes once analyzed as a French mythology return because of the links of language to the grounding of being. The writer attempts to make a cuisine of words, preparing them to appear desirable and intellectually delicious to a reader. From his earliest writing,[38] Barthes admired the Socratic banquet whereby the participants shared dining and conversation, an ideal he mentioned in his preface to Brillat-Savarin.[39] Although Jonathan Culler would have us believe that *jouissance* meant "ease" for Barthes,[40] it was much more likely that, within what Richard Howard calls "an erotics of reading"[41] by Barthes, the word pointed toward an intersection of physical and intellectual apogees where "everything is there, but floating."[42] There would be that symbiotic love of reader for text, a bond that French structuralism began to identify and in which Roland Barthes situated himself as the exemplary reader. The place for that reading would be in the imagination. It was Jacques Lacan, however, who provided the psychoanalytic skills to explain the links of the desire between reader and text. Barthes worked out an ideology for the readerly text from reading the mythologies of society. Meanwhile, Lacan was exposing the underpinnings for a topology of human thinking within French structuralism.

Chapter Four
Lacan and the Purloined Letter

With the publication of *Écrits* in 1966, Jacques Lacan brought psychoanalysis and the structure of the unconscious into the world of French structuralism. Although the title indicates that Lacan's "writings" are to be found here, the irony is that there are none to be found inside: the *Écrits* are transcriptions of Lacan's seminars in Paris. The spoken word of his seminars was displaced and "stolen" or purloined from its intersection with a listening audience watching Lacan perform and dance like a harlequin. The *Écrits* are formidable for any reader because of the heterogeneous essays juxtaposed without context or apparent link. Each essay is an exercise in verbal play and tends to be very dense in its style and argumentation.

The first seminar was an analysis of a literary document: Edgar Allan Poe's "The Purloined Letter," translated by Charles Baudelaire as "La Lettre Volée." Basically, the story is about a letter of unknown content stolen by a minister from his queen and stolen again by a detective Dupin and returned to the queen.

From his insights into the short story, Lacan concluded that the narrative is a conceit for language. Like the purloined letter, language is always missing from its place and always arrives at its destination.[1] On the one hand, language is displaced and condensed from its speaker's intent. On the other hand, language finds its own "reader." At the end of the seminar, Lacan remarked that the letter always arrives at its destination. Given the context of this statement, he was speaking ironically. But Jacques Derrida took him to task for the disjunction between the comment on displacement and the literal sense of the story's conclusion. Derrida proceeded to "deconstruct" and thus to defer Lacan's meaning.[2] Although both Lacan and Derrida were saying that the signifier is constantly being displaced and can never be retrieved, the misunderstanding based on Lacan's written word was another purloined letter exemplifying Lacan's role as the ideologist of the displaced thinking subject. Between Poe and Derrida, literature and philosophy, and narrative and its analysis, Lacan extended the arguments of structural linguistics into the psychoanalytic explorations of the psyche and its social ties.

Lacan learned from both Lévi-Strauss and Barthes. On the one hand,

Lacan's notion of the Symbolic was derived from a Lévi-Strauss essay in 1949 wherein the ethnologist spoke of "the symbolic function"[3] governing the unconscious with universal laws. Lacan would develop this insight into the triadic (the Symbolic, the Imaginary, and the Real) functions by which personality develops. The spoken language fascinated both thinkers. Whereas Lévi-Strauss concentrated on the myths of tribes without literatures, Lacan would become renowned for his "talking cure" (partly a misnomer because he was opposed to the American psychoanalytical approach toward the utility of healing). And both of them tried their talents on literary documents and were rebuffed for not recognizing the differences between writing and speaking.

On the other hand, Roland Barthes, the writer par excellence among the French structuralists, also had interests similar to those of Lacan. As Barbara Johnson has brilliantly developed, the seminar on Poe is an argument for "the letter as its way of reading the act of reading."[4] In effect, Lacan analyzed the components of Barthes's ideology of the readerly text to create an ideology of his own. The coherence of appearances affected both intellectuals. Whereas Barthes spoke about how his desire was often shunted from one mask to another, Lacan's theory of the mirror phase of personality development pointed out that we all go through a phase when we assume that our reflection in a mirror is a sign of the whole subject we claim to be. As with Barthes's masks, however, the unity of the subject is an illusion, according to Lacan. Although Lacan's probe of the mirror phase first appeared in Marienbad in 1936, it was only in 1975 that he revealed the irony of that work by encouraging the study of optics as a way to understand "scientifically" how images are produced.[5]

Both Lacan and Barthes were fond of word play as ways to point out the irony of structure. In the Poe seminar, for example, Lacan referred to "la politique d'Autruiche" (the politics of . . .), playing on the French words for ostrich, others, and Austria to mock Freud's structure of the unconscious as being oblivious to the roles of others in determining the subject. Nevertheless, rather than whole, developed arguments, the literary fragment was a means for both Barthes and Lacan to communicate glimpses of their insights, to be developed by others in the wake of the masters' presence. Lacan even realized part of Barthes's prospectus for the "writerly text,"[6] one whose meaning only the writer could decipher. Lacan's work was displaced from its spoken context, just like the Poe reading. Through the activity of such displacement, Lacan gave us an ideology of the human mind that remains as a testimony to the heritage of French structuralism.

The writings of Lacan have mystified many a reader, even more than those of Lévi-Strauss. Lacan attracted a cult following in Paris from 1953, when he began a splinter group of the International Psychoanalytic Association, until 1980, when he dissolved his school. We will explain his thought by dividing it into five topics: his linguistic model, his postulate of the decentered subject, his triadic construct for personality development, his use of hypnosis, and finally, his feminist influence. Our discussion will move from his observations about language and the unconscious to an explanation of his role as a subversive within the psychoanalytic and French communities.

The Unconscious Structured like a Language

In a conference on structuralism at Johns Hopkins University in 1966, Lacan debated with the sociologist Lucien Goldmann that the unconscious is structured like a language such as English or French.[7] The use of "like" was crucial because structural linguistics gave Lacan the tools to reexamine Freud's thinking subject in language. The linguistic model was important to explore the consequences of Lacan's observation that all humans and their psyches are born in a language. For the psychoanalyst, linguistics is thus a tool for understanding that the moment "in which desire becomes human is also that in which the child is born into language."[8] Jakobson's binary distinctions of metaphor and metonymy exemplify for Lacan that desire is diverted in the psyche through condensation and displacement. Desire thus works through language to implement a chain of signifiers.[9] Meaning is achieved in the subject through this language chain, which erases the referent and the signified of any communication. Hence, psychoanalysis, according to Lacan, cannot use origins or history to help a patient with a given problem. Instead, his practice engaged the analyst and analysand in an experience wherein the id speaks (*ça parle*) through the grammatical form of psychic drives.[10] This active effort to show what language does to the subject recalls Saussure's remark that "language is not a function of the speaker: it is a product that is passively assimilated by the individual."[11]

Displacement and condensation were two functions identified by Freud as structuring the unconscious, the basis for the ego's identity. Rather than as indicators of the unconscious, condensation and displacement were redefined by Lacan as linguistic pointers to the human subject itself as a function. The subject can never be neatly defined as "ego" or "self," according to Lacan. Grammar, the structure of language, constitutes the subject by giving form to the speaking voice. But that "structure" is an elusive one, since the signifier is capable of "sustaining itself only in . . . displacement."[12]

The Saussurian algorithm S/s (Signified/signifier) served as a model for

Lacan's analysis of the role of language in predicating the subject. The position of the bar between the two letters is significant because it represents the one-way passage from the signified to subsequent signifiers; there is no retreat or recovery of the original intent or meaning of the speaker. In addition, the bar represents the gap (*le manque*) within signification or meaning to which Lacan referred throughout his seminars. The unconscious is likewise haunted by a gap waiting to be filled: "The unconscious is this chapter of my life marked by a blank or filled with a lie. It is the censored chapter. But the truth is written elsewhere, specifically in the document the analysand provides to the psychoanalyst."[13] In the document, language provides "the truth," whereby the nature of the unconscious as lie or as blank can be understood. This is not a written document necessarily. The document, however, is "the word of the patient" (the "one medium" of psychoanalysis).[14] This "word" was shared by the analyst and analysand and became the basis for Lacan's seminars. Therein, he reached no conclusions and provided no cures. He demonstrated the linguistic chain of signifiers and thus exemplified the structuralist algorithm within the thinking subject.

The density of Lacan's style allowed him to preempt his readers from premature theory (*le métalangage*). Some of Lacan's readers admit that his style is impossible to master and to understand completely. This very admission leads to the conclusion stated by Jane Gallop as "everyone's inevitable 'castration' in language."[15] That is, the human subject loses self-control within the continuous chain of signifiers. Lacan's impenetrable style demonstrates the illusion of control the subject has in an assumed mastery of any knowledge. His plays on words and dense style appear to be almost impenetrable at times and frustrating if one is expecting high-flown theoretical pronouncements. Let us recall that his written texts were purloined, displaced, and condensed versions of his seminars, where many students had been mesmerized by the power of his presence. Stuart Schneiderman, a professor of English at SUNY-Buffalo, resigned his faculty position to become a witness to Lacan's "shows" (see his testimony, *Jacques Lacan: The Death of an Intellectual Hero,* 1983). One of Lacan's students, Catherine Clément, writes in her biography of Lacan that, in his seminars, he "does not really make the connection between the poetic and the pathological: he dances about, he behaves seductively."[16]

Lacan's slippery and seductive behavior was in part due to the influence of Émile Benveniste's linguistic studies. Benveniste studied pronouns in the various Indo-European languages and concluded that pronouns are locutions and not substitutes for "reality."[17] The ego is already constituted as the subject in language, so that pronouns become ways of presenting this subject from different angles. Benveniste distinguished between the subject of a statement (*l'énoncé*) and what is being said (*l'énonciation*). This distinction proved to be appropriate for Lacan's formulation of the subject as function. For example, Lacan noted that the statement "I am lying" is an admission of a moral action and a constitution of the thinking subject. Only the Other can see the duplicity of this thinking subject using and being used by language.

The Rejection of *Homo Psychologicus*

Louis Althusser noted that Lacan's work demonstrated the assumptions on which Freud based his theory: the denial of the myth of *homo psychologicus*.[18] This myth had been created by the ego psychologists. From Descartes to Freud, the ego psychologists developed the thinking subject as a definable whole, capable of being constituted, analyzed, and layered (e.g., ego, superego, id). This perspective, which has been augmented in the twentieth century by the American behavioral influences of B. F. Skinner and the American structuralist classification schemes of Leonard Bloomfield, has been promoted in the recent past by the depth psychologists Heinz Hartmann, Rudolf Leowenstein, and Ernst Kris. Lacan was certainly opposed to the assumption that ego was the central focus of human behavior. Ego psychologists assumed that humanity possessed verifiable centers of cognitive activity known as egos. This "humanistic" frame of mind implied that the subject exists from the very beginning of human life. Jean Piaget, who assessed French structuralism in 1968, belonged to this ego-centered weltanschauung. Lacan detected the "Piagetic [*sic*] error,"[19] whereby the egocentric child's discourse was a basis for the structures of cognitive development.

Instead, Lacan developed a view of the subject as a function of the Other. This subject is a thinking person whose identity is in constant flux, wavering dialectically between the self and the mirror-image perception of self as Other. From the "mirror phase" of development, the child learns about modeling the self on that reflection in the mirror. The "mirror phase" was a Lacanian interpretation of the Freudian observation that the child reacts to the first object it sees by distinguishing between here and there (*fort/da* in German) and thus creating the topology for the rest of its psychological life. Whereas the "whole" person appears in a mirror, the distinction between here and there begins a disjunctive separation of self and Other, effectively splitting the subject and causing it to vacillate permanently in search of that "whole person" it once saw and continues to see in the mirror. The disjunction is a basic division of being (the German *Spaltung*), marking the subject's struggles throughout its psychological life.

This division of being begins with the child's struggles between itself and the first outside object it sees. That object enables the child to distinguish its mother, through which its identity is involved in transference of self, from something totally Other. In that *fort/da* struggle, narrated by Freud as the child's perception of a spool of thread falling away from the crib, Lacan proposed the subject as intimately linked with its language. In Lacan's "Discourse at Rome" in 1953 when he first separated from the International Psychoanalytical Association (IPA), he articulated these views of "Freud's talking cure." In effect, Lacan set out to demonstrate a Freud despite himself, a Freud whose works show a genius other than what he consciously intended. The Saussurian insight into the components of language as *langue,* the cultural and communal properties learned from others, and *parole,* the innate skill to communicate, is especially pertinent to Lacan's reading of Freud. The division of being, or *Spaltung,* originated from the inherent problem of language: being caught up in a struggle between the self and others. We use a language, which belongs to others, in a personal desire to communicate.

Lacan insisted that there can be no "here" (*fort*) without a "there" (*da*).[20] By this statement, he meant that the human subject is constantly caught up in the endless repetition of the object of transference (*objet petit "a"*: the other as object). The self is in a continual struggle with alienation from objects outside itself. As a child, the objects may be the mother's breast, feces, the human gaze, the human voice; all these objects represent for the child a sense of otherness. For the adult, the child's predicament in the mirror stage evolves into the separation of the self in the mirror from the omnipresent Other. Lacan saw his position there: "I am unable to see myself from the place where the Other is looking at me."[21]

Triangulating the Model

Lacan triangulated the binary models provided by structural linguistics for understanding language. Self and other were dialectical points of departure for understanding human personalities. They were also involved, however, in a double bind. From the Freudian Oedipus complex, Lacan proposed a tertium quid: the father. The father is the other who interrupts the transference between mother and child and forever remains as part of the human psyche to triangulate the self. Whereas Freud had naively structured the subject in components identified as the id, the ego, and the superego, Lacan elaborated three complex types of activity similarly imbedded in the subject: the pre-conscious, the unconscious, and the conscious. The time element of "pre-conscious" is significant because it denotes time (cf. Martin Heidegger's

Being and Time, 1927) as a major influence on the *Spaltung* or division in the psychological life of the subject.

The presence of values associated with the father is the basis for identifying the influence of phallocentrism. While the mother and child are bonding in a mutual sense of fascination, the father enters with a jarring sense of otherness for the child. Whether or not the father is still alive does not matter to Lacan, because cultural prejudice is so informed by the presence of the father's otherness that the subject cannot escape its effects. Lacan invented his own terminology to speak of what the father means in the development of the subject. He spoke of the law of the symbolic to convey the pervasive psychological pattern imposed by the father.

The law of the symbolic triangulates what Lacan distinguished as the real and the imaginary realms of knowledge. This triadic configuration is an abstraction of the trinity, within which the father is placed at the hierarchically superior apex. It is the power of symbols to create a geometry of the tension between the self and others. Lacan went further and indicated that the structure of the self entailed a topographical study, a mapping of the various components of the psyche in search of itself. Of course, the "topoi" or places must be specially defined because the subject is not a locus. The subject is on an odyssey in which the real, the imaginary, and the symbolic triangulate the movement from within and create three poles magnetically attracting the conscious.

This triadic structure of the subject avoids the hierarchic pitfalls of the ego psychologists by deferring power to the subject. In ego psychology, the strong ego of the analyst overwhelms the weak ego of the analysand because the analyst is in the hierarchically superior power position as the one who knows. Lacan instead participated in the patient's struggle with the other. By avoiding the ego psychologist's role as what Anthony Wilden calls "the symbol hunter,"[22] Lacan demonstrated the work of the symbolic in creating patterns of what was the law, the right, authority, and culture as incarnated in the father. These absolute terms compose a "phallogocentric" language and psyche.

This law of the symbolic entails the imposition of human order on behavior through a rational code of what right, law, culture, and authority signify. They represent the judgments of others on the formation of the self as the child develops into adulthood. While the child's language is imbued with the presence of the father, language becomes "phallogocentric." The phallus is the maypole around which the child and the mother wrap their ribbons of self.

Feminists in France, since 1968, especially the group "Psych et Po" with

the logo MLF (Mouvement de Libération des Femmes), have been especially influenced, through Hélène Cixous (b. 1937) and Luce Irigaray (b. 1939), to seek a third position, one that is not polarized as either male or female.[23] Irigaray, a Lacanian psychoanalyst expelled from the École freudienne de Paris for her feminist challenges in a book entitled *Speculum,* asserted that "in *Speculum* I try to go back through the masculine imaginary, to interpret how it has reduced us to silence, to mutism, to imitation, and I try, from there, and at the same time, to (re)find a possible space for a feminine imaginary."[24] Within the triangulation of the psyche, she thus hopes to work out a nonhierarchical place for women's identity. The major problem is that the symbolic law, according to Lacan, is at the pinnacle of the triangle, as society understands the father: the incarnation of the word and reason, as well as authority, culture, law, and right. Lacan has thus managed to inspire revolutionary work among feminists to upset the phallogocentric discourse of a logocentric Western society. He pointed out the ties between language and the father's role in triangulating the psyche with the law of the symbolic.

Fluidity is also essential in the triangular structure of the real, the imaginary, and the symbolic. Just as the subject is portrayed in a struggle with the other to find what the self means, so the abstract principles governing this struggle are constantly vacillating, depending on the apparent fixations of a given moment in time. As opposed to the IPA's portrayal of Freudian analysis as a search for past events to explain present behavior, Lacan preferred to look forward in his triangulation of the psyche. He specifically focused on the future anterior tense of verbs as indicative of the formative struggles of the psyche in the present. He noted in the *Écrits* that the analyst should be aware that the patient's history reveals not so much the past as "the future anterior of what I will have been for what I am in the process of becoming."[25] This formation of the subject is thus fragmented. And the picture puzzle emerges as a model for the assembly of the subject continually in the throes of constructing, destructing, and reconstructing itself.

Truth as a Psychological Rebus

Of course, Lacan was always the only one who could play at this game of the picture puzzle. He was only comfortable as the authority figure who told others what the psyche was about. He kept his listeners, and now his readers, at bay by using a deliberately ambiguous and often polyvalent style. It was and is disconcerting to try and find a theoretically coherent truth within his seminars. And yet that was exactly his message: that knowledge itself is constructed in an ad hoc fashion. Although Lacan disagreed with Freud's conscious point of departure that the subject is certain and identifiable, the French psychoanalyst marvels at chapter 6 of Freud's *The Interpretation of Dreams*, wherein the rebus or picture puzzle is presented as a model for the analysis of the unconscious. The fragmentation of the subject was in fact demonstrated by Freud's partition of the ego, superego, and id. Lacan then focused on this fragmentation and spoke of the pieces rather than a wholly assembled puzzle. The stylistic literary fragments preferred in the self-reflective writings of Lacan, as well as in those of Roland Barthes, convey a sympathetic sensitivity to the dissolving subject in their form. The cracks separating the pieces of the rebus are real ones and represent the possibility for the dissolution of the assembled pieces from time to time. And so it is with knowledge, as the subject collects pieces of information.

Some would have Lacan arguing for "the circularity of discourse."[26] But the redundancy of the circle retracing a pattern upon itself is too naive. The subject indeed recirculates information previously encountered, but in a fragmented way. The subject constructs the patterns, but the subject also grows and changes as it struggles with the Other within the triangular structure. The circular pattern of discourse assumes that Truth is complete and closed in nature.

Perhaps a better model for Lacanian discourse is the spiral,[27] whereby the circle is part of a series capable of change yet also accommodating a similarity in structure. The triangular network could then work within each spire such that the Symbolic would not be structurally superior as the pinnacle but merely one of the three components of the thinking subject.

Freud's conception of the subject's structure had implied a layering of planes of psychic activity according to each of the components (id, ego, and superego). The spiral model for the psyche allows fluidity from spire to spire without the layers being fixed in extension. Lacan, having been the director of the clinic at the Paris Faculté de Médecine in 1932, was certainly aware that psychoanalysis was claiming to be a science, with pretensions of mathematical verification. In this role, it sought to isolate its concerns empirically. Lacan shook those beliefs to ask "whether psychoanalysis is a science."[28] He doubted that it was possible to verify the existence of the subject and to dissect its activities into different planes. Rather than "analysis," whereby the analyst assumes a position of knowing the unity of another subject as a discrete whole, Lacan presented hypnosis as the means to discover that "this crossing of the plane of identification is possible."[29]

The hope for hypnosis, rather than analysis, appears to some of Lacan's critics as more structuralist obfuscation. For example, Richard Harland understands Lacan's concern with hypnosis "as though he must at all costs paper over the cracks and incoherences in his façade of unity."[30]

But Lacan was also showing cracks where unity had been assumed. In his topography of the mind, he identified a redistribution of the identifiable masses according to different shapes with boundaries different from those previously acknowledged by psychoanalysis. For Lacan there were four fundamental problems to be addressed by psychoanalysis: the unconscious, repetition, drives, and transference. All of these are interwoven in the experience of hypnosis, that mesmerizing activity similar to what Lacan himself achieved in his seminars. He laid open the unconscious by lulling consciousness to sleep since his arguments could not be followed logically. The control he exerted over his disciples (Clément spoke of "the Lacan Affair . . . as if he had never been anything but a splendid clown, a guru *de luxe* for Parisian intellectuals"[31]) exemplified the transference between analyst and analysand. His talking cures spoke about repetition and drives as the apparent subjects, and yet he insisted on controlling the subject matter. The hypnosis entailed Lacan the Father dazzling with his own symbolic system.

Since his first separation from the IPA in 1953, Lacan had announced his subversive voice and renounced collective rule. Despite his own past as director of psychoanalysis at the Paris Faculté de Médecine, he criticized the professional association for being anti-intellectual because of "the segregation of psychiatry in the Faculté de Médecine where the university structure displays its affinities with the managerial system."[32] Throughout his career, he led various psychoanalytic groups to be avant-garde or subversive in their approach to the psyche and to the practice of psychoanalysis itself (e.g., his advocacy of "the short session" and the pass, two associations produced between regularly scheduled sessions with a patient).[33] The final coup came in 1980 when he dissolved his School in a very formal, official manner because, as his biographer Clément remarked, "when Lacan's words had circulated far too widely, when they became not his words but the words of his School, he dissolved the School."[34] He realized that the adjective "Lacanian" had become formulaic and that he could no longer control his presence as the Father. It was during that period that Alice Cherki told him that a group of psychoanalysts in Caracas were studying his texts without the talking cure from Lacan himself. He became resigned and replied: "It interests me to know what happens when my person no longer screens what I teach."[35] This insight shows the struggle that he also experienced with his self and the other, as reflected in his using the first and third person forms within the same sentence.

The Subversion of Phallogocentrism

Phallogocentrism is the symbolic role of the phallus at the core of human discourse. The absence of the phallus, because the penis is usually sheathed and hidden from view, creates a desire within language to express what is latent or deliberately concealed. Lacan's seminars were elaborations of the effects of this problem to express in language the psychological drives associated with hiding or revealing the phallus. The triadic structure of the personality was likewise involved with this phenomenon. Lacan, playing the role of the father in his seminars, maintained the authoritative and hierarchical position of hiding or showing the phallus whenever his desires were so moved. In effect, the ambiguities of his own discourse necessitated his intervention to control the nature of truth (the phallus) by correcting others when they provided the "wrong" interpretations of his ambiguities or by encouraging those who elaborated upon his texts in a manner acceptable to him. Serge Leclaire and Jacques-Alain Miller, for example, were usually allowed to present "properly" the doctrines of Lacan. But Lacan was very careful not to endorse "unauthorized," that is, uncontrolled, versions (e.g., the feminist writings of Luce Irigaray and Jane Gallop).

And yet the feminists contributed the most significant elaborations of Lacanian psychoanalysis to survive out of French structuralism. Lacan's panoply of elaborations about phallogocentrism now seems utterly ironic, because the clearly misogynistic tone of his lectures contrasts with the inspiration of some of his female disciples, such as Clément, who asserts that "in Lacan I recognize myself as a Frenchwoman."[36] That recognition has spawned many a reaction in feminist circles to change the situation of phallogocentrism. Lacan was not simply misogynistic. Rather he was indicating the phallocentric condition of language in determining patterns of thinking.

Lacan pointed out that "the father's name" brings with it the psychological traits of the entry into the symbolic. Women are thus constantly menaced by identification with a sex not their own and must struggle with the overbearing presence of the father in their lives. Lacan used a sentence to exemplify this situation of woman: "Ce n'est pas lui, mon père" ("He's not the one, Father" and/or "That's not my father"). The ambiguity of the sentence is characteristic of Lacan's style and the presence of the symbolic. Distinguishing the man from the father may be impossible, whether or not the father is present.

Freudian psychoanalysts have traditionally called this phenomenon the castration complex. Feminists, however, have learned from Lacan that the status of the phallus is a fraud.[37] The phallus or the power of the father is in his absence, to recall the desire for the place of the other. Thus, desire can be expressed as a want and also as a lack of the other. The triangulation of the personality has the effect of creating a place for the father by breaking the duality of mother-child so insisted on in the research of Melanie Klein (1882–1960) and rediscovered by Julia Kristeva and her *chora*.[38] But the hierarchical place given to the father in the Symbolic refers women to a language whereby the phallus (i.e., truth) is given a mysterious, cloaked aura. Although Freud had given psychoanalysis the program that "does not try to describe what a woman is—that would be a task it could scarcely perform—but sets about enquiring how she comes into being,"[39] woman is relegated in terms of the father's law of the symbolic rather than in her own terms. Her own being is ignored as she must use the Other's language. Lacan even said that "LA femme (THE Woman) can only be written by crossing through LA: there is no LA FEMME, no definite article to designate the universal."[40] Language and the symbolic thus worked together to absorb women into discourse.

Lacan provided insight into subverting the power of the phallus in discourse. Since "the phallus can only play its role when veiled,"[41] the game is then to reveal that truth in its naked absence. Silence in the past implied respect for the law of the father. Leclaire developed Lacan's thoughts to remark that transference of this law is achieved from the father to women because of the lack of response to its situation of Law, Right, or Order.[42] Hence, feminists are inspired to respond to Lacan and to expose the phallus for its fraudulent representation of truth and language. Jacqueline Rose incisively comments that Lacan's often-missed lesson is that "the subject's entry into the symbolic order is equally an exposure of the phallus itself."[43] In other words, once the power of the law of the symbolic is revealed, we must recognize the validity of Saussure's observation that "speech always implies both an established system and an evolution."[44] Rather than looking backward into the past as traditional psychoanalysis teaches, Lacan thus encouraged recognizing the father's role as part of the psyche's preconscious and subverting its authoritative position in personality development.

Lacan's psychoanalysis remains today as a testimony to understanding readers as both analysts and analysands. Shoshana Felman has demonstrated that Lacanian reading is both a "relation of interpretation" by an analyst and a "relation of transference" learned by the text's authority over a patient or reader.[45] Lacan himself was analyst and patient in that he was the father controlling the interpretations of his seminars and also the subject being deployed by the ambiguity of his lectures. Since he understood the phallus to be "the index for the missing letter"[46] (also "desire for the letter" and "absence of the letter"), we return to the focus of the seminar from which he began: the purloined letter. Language itself is purloined (condensed and displaced) as the "truth" of the unconscious is deferred upon successive folds of the signifier.

Jacques Derrida's program for "deconstruction" succeeded in displacing Lacan's effect by dismantling the basis for the psychoanalyst's insights, Poe's short story. Derrida accused Lacan of ignoring the narrative voice in "The Purloined Letter" and not realizing that the narrator and Dupin were voices doubling each other.[47] The story was not about the displacement of the ego and the questioning of the utility of healing, but rather how narrating voices narrate.

Derrida's comment on Lacan's work has brought to light the importance of recognizing Lacan's voice as representative of a desire for power. Lacan ignored the narrative voices of the written story because he sought to impose the authority of his own spoken delivery, whose tone and presence are lost in a written document. Although he often stressed the importance of *mi-dire* (speaking in half-truths), he did not ever suggest that his own power as the father should be questioned because he did not possess the whole "truth." And yet, at the end of his School in 1980, he became a tragic father-figure, like King Lear, as Schneiderman observed.[48] For example, Lacan tried to displace Foucault's analysis of the play with perspectives in the painting *Las Meñinas* (1656). Lacan shifted the focus of the painting to an explanation of what was totally hidden: the genitals of the Infanta.[49] But no one was listening to Lacan's response to Foucault. Instead, Foucault's revelation that the perspectives in *Las Meñinas* are governed by the power of its language subverted the authority of Lacan's own phallogocentric discourse. Rather than the dogmatic presence of the Father, society's ideological stakes in language had to be exposed. Michel Foucault did such an exposition and thus allowed the exponents of French structuralism to be criticized and superseded by the larger contextual setting of communication.

Chapter Five

Foucault and the Revelation of Power

Trained as a philosopher and a psychologist, Michel Foucault brought the "human sciences" into a dialogue about the problems Western civilization had wrought by acknowledging Nietzsche's dictum that "God is dead." His identification with French structuralism began with the publication of his *Les Mots et les choses* (*The Order of Things*) in 1966 and *L'Archéologie du savoir* (*The Archaeology of Knowledge*) in 1969, wherein he presented the practices of language as paradigms for social and political weltanschauungen. Although he began his career with suspicions that Saussure's *langue* contained hidden structures linking power and knowledge in society, Foucault's work evolved toward a semiotic sensitivity for the social and political manifestations of power relationships. Language always preoccupied his writings, but with shifts of priority as he became increasingly curious about the role played by the silences of languages in history.

Foucault was concerned with how transformations occurred in history with the presence of so many discontinuities (*coupures*) ignored by traditional history. This traditional history, for Foucault, is specifically exposed as a "history of events" (*l'historie événementielle*),[1] with its sequence of past-present-future, the assumption of progress, or a unidirectional evolutionary scheme totalizing a subject as a consistent whole. Instead, Foucault sought to explain the unthinkable, because the rejected, ignored, or pariahs of social history could tell us about the power relationships created by the discontinuities of arbitrary distinctions among a society's members. During his career, he was especially concerned with the insane, the sick, imprisoned criminals, and the sexually deviant, as groups whose voices had been silent in history and whose social isolation revealed connections between power and knowledge.

The problem of historical discontinuities was not conceived by Foucault in a vacuum. During the 1930s and 1940s, Gaston Bachelard (1884–1962) had spoken about the history of science and how the sciences had to say no to the past in order to evolve. In 1966, the American Thomas Kuhn (b. 1922) theorized in his *The Structure of Scientific Revolutions* that the scientific models of "paradigms" were breaks in "normal science," unable to adapt to anomalies encountered by the scientific perspective in vogue at the time. Meanwhile, in the social sciences, Fernand Braudel (1902–85) and Louis Althusser had discussed discontinuities and history. Braudel was a proponent of the *Annales* School of history, as begun in the 1930s by Marc Bloch (1886–1944) and Lucien Febvre (1878–1956). In Braudel's 1949 study *La Méditerranée et le Monde méditerranéan à l'époque de Philippe II*, he proposed a geohistory "to see on a grand scale"[2] across the limits of individual lives and events. The second edition of this work appeared in 1966, when it was also translated into English. Althusser, who was Foucault's teacher at the École Normale Supérieure, argued in 1965 in *Pour Marx* (see chapter 6) that there was an "epistemological break" in the mid-nineteenth century, whereby idealism and materialism could no longer be reconciled, as is reflected in the writings of Karl Marx. And so Foucault began his career in an intellectual climate of suspicion about the discontinuities in history.

In many ways, Foucault can be understood to have developed some of Lacan's ideas in psychoanalysis. Indeed, historical discontinuities were generally not consciously contrived to build power relationships. The human sciences, as the social sciences are generally known in France, did not have a method to explain the working of the unconscious. Through his study of psychology, Foucault entered the realm of psychoanalysis. With his training in the analytical tools of philosophy, he saw the hope offered by psychoanalysis: "Whereas all the human sciences advance toward the unconscious with their back to it, waiting for it to unveil itself as fast as consciousness is analysed, psychoanalysis, on the other hand, points directly towards it . . . towards what exists with the mute solidity of a thing, of a text closed in upon itself, or of a blank space in a visible text."[3] This latter allusion was especially appropriate for Foucault's method, because he set out to make visible those connections, or structures, in history unseen by others.

The Symbolic Law of the unconscious—identified by Lacan with authority, order, and hegemony—became a fertile area to be examined by Foucault. He rejected the tendencies in psychoanalysis to recover a genesis, a continuity with the past, or a totalization of the subject. He bemoaned the fact that traditional history assumed that the subject could synthesize and be synthesized. Similar to Lévi-Strauss, Barthes, and Lacan, who announced the end of humanism as it was conceived prior to French structuralism, Foucault resuscitated Nietzsche to observe that "rather than the death of God, what Nietzsche's thought heralds is the end of his murderer."[4] Without God, there is no Man. The study of humanism assumed that Man was a universal value coterminous with God. Foucault discovered that humanism was hiding human desire by containing "everything in Western civilization that restricts the desire for power."[5] By discovering that Man was not a legitimate concept, he exposed the bankruptcy of humanism as it had been conceived prior to French structuralism. Likewise, the relations among people in society had to be reexamined in light of this discovery. In effect, the modern sensibility, which Foucault understood as beginning with Freud and Saussure, involved Foucault's own agenda, especially as portrayed by Karlis Racevski: "to recuperate, to colonize, to disenfranchise the Symbolic in the name of a ratio."[6]

The ratio or logic was called "archaeology" in the early writings of Foucault. It would evolve into "genealogy" and eventually "topology." His choice of terms to describe his methods reflected the development of his vision from the structuralist concern with form (archaeology) through a period of concern with patterns (genealogy) to a panoramic conjunction of space and time (topology). Archaeology was clearly allied with history and also with structuralism. Lévi-Strauss had called geology one of his three inspirations in that it was a model for his probing the substrata of appearances. The major "ideologists" of French structuralism all referred to the disparity between appearances and substance. Their "ideologies," for the most part, revealed the structures of the substances lurking beneath or on the other side of deceptive appearances. Foucault, however, distinguished himself here, too, because he often began with an appearance that didn't "belong" or was inconsistent with other appearances. He looked for the "tip of the iceberg" as a point of departure for his exposés.

During his fascination with archaeology, Foucault would often begin his studies with an artifact, for example, the painting *Las Meñinas* by Velázquez (1599–1660), and then demonstrate how it was an anomaly to its historical setting, as traditionally conceived. From that artifact or event, he then developed his archaeology as "the history of that which renders necessary a certain form of thought."[7] His style generally was to find an example of a pariah in a particular society and then to discuss the parameters for the exclusion of that individual in a class.

The 1968 student riots were a key moment in French structuralism. The word "structuralist" was identified with DeGaulle's administration and a compartmentalized and dated university educational system in France. Foucault was in Tunisia during that period of unrest and returned to become the chair of the Department of Philosophy at the University of Vincennes, a campus newly created to respond to the 1968 crisis. These political events influenced the intellectual focus of Foucault's work. He began denying his affiliation with structuralism and admitted his mania for forms in his earlier works. His method began to be identified with "genealogy," effectively breaking his association with his earlier structuralist colleagues by this change in vocabulary. Rather than continue in his structuralist concerns with language and Cartesian epistemology, he adopted "genealogy" as his method to refer to the systems or patterns of family trees in the history of ideas. Within these systems, he then began to chart specific directions and referred to his method as "topology," thus identifying his role as a cartographer charting previously unexplored intellectual fields.

Foucault's procession from archaeology to topology is the organizing thread for our presentation of his work. He was a French structuralist aware of the limitations of structuralism, with a vision to its displacement by a semiotics able to look at a context larger than that of discourse. After presenting his discovery of the silences of history, I will discuss his proposal for epistemic systems, the politics of power, the fields of discontinuities, and the geography of history.

In the Margins of History

Traditional history had been unable to speak about discontinuities. It relegated society's pariahs to silence after they were shut up in asylums (the insane), teaching clinics (the sick who were indigent), or prisons of one sort or another (criminals, homosexuals, and others judged to be "deviant"). Economic history revealed that these pariahs were thus taken out of capitalistic systems and effectively rendered powerless because they had not been playing efficient economic roles in their respective societies. The social discourses about these people and events were then excluded from the domain of "the history of events." For Foucault, these very discourses thus became hidden repositories to study the connections between power and knowledge: "Taking the discourse itself, its appearances, and its regularity, we should look for its external conditions of existence, for that which gives rise to the chanceries of these events and fixes its limits."[8] In the process of examining these chanceries and their limits, he put together a history that was antihistorical. Hayden White, one of the few professional historians to appreciate Foucault initially, said it well: "Foucault writes 'history' in order to destroy it as a discipline, as a mode of consciousness, and as a mode of (social) existence."[9]

What Foucault did write was a critique of society's self-perceptions as reflected in its choices of who belongs and who doesn't. These choices are found in the discourses of its representatives. The medical profession came under his scrutiny first as it locked away the insane in asylums and relegated the indigent sick to teaching clinics where either group would be less taxing on the financial resources of society at large. Foucault went on to point out how the discourse of medicine had rendered invisible the mad (unreasonable) and the sick who were indigent.

His *Naissance de la clinique* (*The Birth of the Clinic*) in 1963 was subtitled "An archaeology of medical perception." And indeed, the medical profession's perception had been so limited as to cause some persons to disappear for the economic benefit of the majority class the medical doctors elected to "cure." Foucault indicated that "this book is about space, about language, and about death: it is about the act of seeing, the gaze."[10]

From Maurice Blanchot (b. 1907), Foucault learned that the gaze [11] was an informative source of inclusion and exclusion. In Foucault's *Les Mots et les choses*, he described *Las Meñinas* as the greatest painting in the world because it acts as a mirror to make us question the very act of looking at the painting and what it is that we see when we look. Traditional history ("the history of events"), on the other hand, sought to recover a human event in time and space and to reconstitute a story around that event. Similar in many respects to the linguistics-inspired studies of Lévi-Strauss, Foucault's early interest in binary analysis[12] was instrumental in his intersected visions of history. By intersecting his own gaze (he readily admitted being caught up in the modern way of looking) with that of the doctors, the jurists, the economists, and other social scientists, he projected phenomenological ways of understanding history. These phenomenological ways or methods were outside what was usually accepted as "history." Indeed, Foucault's work was initially rejected as history by many English and American historians.[13] Foucault's concerns with epistemology and phenomenology were properly philosophical and did not corroborate the established canon of historical periods.

Instead, Foucault was beginning his lifelong analysis of the disruptions rather than the continuities of history within the accepted parameters for what constituted history. By not accepting the myths of progress, genesis, or continuity, Foucault had already placed himself in the margins of established history. The stakes became greater when he began to reduce the human sciences to their discourses and to the games played by their speakers and their listeners. The discourses of the human sciences revealed the gazes of both players. Through Foucault's analyses of the games found in these discourses, he proposed to find the intersections of the gazes and therein the paradigms for social, economic, and political adhesion as yet unthought. But there was the rub for historians reading this philosopher-psychologist: he proposed that by a series of analogies and successions, history could be explained by systems of unthought. Foucault would thus displace the history of ideas with "épistemès" transcending time and place.

Archaeology and Knowledge

In *Les Mots et les choses*, Foucault advanced the possibility of retracing the evolution of the human sciences. With his archaeological method, he probed the fertile soil of how each science organized knowledge. While he was doing this, he rejected the historical periods of "the history of events" and noted that, nevertheless, there were common criteria whereby knowledge was derived within certain space-time restrictions. (Once again, Bakhtin's term "chronotope"[14] is a very good rendering of this grid.)

Foucault identified four of these space-time grids, called "épistemès": the Renaissance (late Middle Ages to late Renaissance), the Classical (seventeenth and eighteenth centuries), the Modern (1785 to the early twentieth century), and the Postmodern (from Freud and Saussure to its still evolving condition). The space for each was Western Europe. Each épistemè had its own discourse with its own parameters alternating between analogy and succession to relate words and things. Richard Rorty tells us that these épistemès presented us with a "theory of how objects constitute themselves in discourse."[15] But even more profound is the systems of meanings for these various constitutions of words and things. Each épistemè entailed discursive ties between knowledge and power.

Some of the integrity in the épistemès was traced back to the institutional control of discourse. In his 1970 inaugural lecture (*L'Ordre du discours, The Order of Discourse*) to the Collège de France, Foucault invented a voice providing the institutional response to an individual's need to communicate by noting the political significance of Saussure's *langue / parole*: "You don't have to worry about beginning. We are all here to show you that discourse is in the scheme of laws; that we have been watching over its presence for a long time; that it has a reserved position which honors and yet disarms it; and that, if it happens to have any power, the power comes from us and from us only and resides in discourse."[16] Who is this institutionalized "us"? Sounds rather like Big Brother. But Foucault was not so concerned with the voice of the future moment as he was with disguised past voices and the rules by which these voices interwove power and knowledge.

Foucault went as far back as the Renaissance, when words were assumed to resemble things, to note and admire Don Quixote. Since Quixote realized that words could wander off on their own, without content or resemblances to things, he was a precursor of Saussure's arbitrary signifier and Freud's unconscious power of language in the modern épistemè. This épistemè began in the early twentieth century and represents the breakdown of phenomenological assumptions about the subject's apprehension of knowledge. These assumptions can be traced back to a Renaissance world order and to Descartes's originating subject in the classical épistemè and developed further by the Enlightenment. Although Foucault described three major epistemological shifts in Western civilization, his program for these shifts has never been completely verified. Piaget even accused Foucault of being too idiosyncratic because the épistemès were "historical apriorities."[17] In fact, Foucault barely sketched the outlines for these épistemès. His whole work was not dependent on this loose end, however. The épistemès are simply part of his paradigmatic way of understanding history. They are valuable for the larger questions that they cause us to ask about why history is ordered as it is today. These questions have to do with how ethics has been replaced by politics, why certain groups are silenced by selected dominant discourses in society, and how we can convert political opposition into semiotic exchange. "Semiotic exchange" is the active communication with, rather than the silencing of, the disenfranchised.

The meanings of the words *discourse* and *power* were seminal in the procession of Foucault's epistemological studies. It was through "discourse" that he sought to examine the relationships between "power" and knowledge. The word *discourse* was broadly used to refer to any language system in which consistent patterns of usage created communities of discontinuities or pariahs. The potential to create these communities of outcasts exists in systems of language. This potential is different than the "power" Foucault discovered. In *L'Histoire de la sexualité*, he notes that power is a "complex strategical situation in a particular society."[18] It is also a relationship for him, so that the word "structure" is especially appropriate to describe Foucault's view of power. Whereas some contemporaries compare Foucault's studies of power to the dialectic of *Vernunft und Herrschaft* (Reason and domination) promoted by the Frankfurt School's Habermas and Gadamer,[19] Foucault's structure of power as a relationship was not perceived by him as the dominant voice of an institution such as the Collège de France, where he taught from 1970 until his death in 1984. Of course, Gadamer's objection to Habermas, that an enlightened observer also tyrannizes, by the use of incisive reasoning to lead the masses against a previously unknown tyrannical power, also characterizes Foucault's own discourse.

Another seminal concept in Foucault's repertoire is what he meant by "knowledge." The knowledge that interested Foucault was information imposed by the hegemony of a privileged few to exclude certain groups of people. For example, when asylums were first conceived as places to dispense with madness by isolating it from the community of reasoned discourse, the medical practitioner was the guardian of reason with "his absolute authority in the world of the asylum . . . insofar as, from the beginning, he was Father and Judge, Family and Law—his medical practice being for a long time no more than a complement to the old rites of Order, Authority, and Punishment."[20] The Symbolic Law, identified by Lacan as having such an imposing presence in the constitution of the unconscious mind, was historically operative in the medical profession's decisions about what was sane and insane discourse and behavior.

Piaget, a trained biologist who became a developmental psychologist, spurned Foucault's archaeological need to look for meanings in the margins of everyday life for the majority of people: "What Foucault forgets is that the whole of cognitive life is linked to structures which are just as unconscious as the Freudian Id, but which reconnect knowledge with life in general."[21] And yet Piaget also ignored Foucault's commentary that we must get outside of ourselves to know ourselves better.

It is questionable whether Foucault succeeded in getting outside the epistemological systems he was trying to describe as dominant and exclusive ideologies. Jean Baudrillard wrote a brilliant critique of Foucault as basically trapped within the Classical épistemè because "Foucault's discourse is a mirror of the power it describes."[22] What we see in reading Foucault is thus a hall of mirrors: his discourse reflects the visual games of perspective being played out in the Classical épistemè, whereby "the sovereign act of nomination"[23] governs society and its pariahs. Foucault assumed that, because he named a certain epistemological system, it had existed.

In a more mature phase of his career (after 1969), Foucault became aware of the naiveté in "the illusion of autonomous discourse"[24] represented by the épistemès and thus the limitations of his own arguments. In an interview with Lucette Finas, he was especially perceptive about the relationships between fiction and knowledge in his own work: "I am well aware that I have never written anything but fictions. I do not mean that fictions are outside of truth. I think it is possible to make fiction work within truth, to produce truthful effects with a fictional discourse. . . . History becomes fiction based on a political reality that makes it true, a future political reality becomes fiction based on historical truth."[25] As a writer of "fictions," Foucault thus admitted that in his own discourse, there was an intersection among truth, historical events, and political power. His épistemès were not as objective as he had intended them to be. But, by admitting the presence of "fictions" therein, he introduced the idea of subversion, as a criterion not only of his discourse but of social discourses throughout history.

The Political Subversion of Power

Foucault spans the bridge between French structuralism and poststructuralism. Whereas he joined other French structuralists in noting the power of language, he went further by daring to look at the subversion of that very power through political struggle. He had first broached the subject of subversion by daring to criticize Soviet ideology in 1961 in his *Folie et déraison* (*Madness and Civilization*). Although Foucault had left the French Communist Party in 1950, his criticism of Soviet farm policy was a daring move because the French Communist Party (PCF), whose sympathizers and members comprised a large segment of the intellectuals who would read Foucault, was still an adjunct to the Soviet party in 1961.

Foucault substituted politics as a viable explanation of human action for the morality extinguished by Nietzsche's pronouncement of the "death of God." The power of politics was concentrated in the strategies of institutions, like the Soviet Politburo's surreptitious regulation of farm production during the 1930s, despite its dominant voice speaking about the collective good of the Communist political system. Here, Foucault saw the death of Man and the concomitant rebirth of political strategies to control individuals through secretive, hegemonic practices.

Criticism is not the same as subversion, however. The conjunction of knowledge and power (*savoir/pouvoir*) is also achieved in Foucault's own discourse as he subverts the secret accumulation of knowledge by making known the hidden relationships between the two in other discourses. Foucault's early works criticized the power of certain discourses to create social outcasts and thus discontinuities or anomalies within communities. Fredric Jameson, however, pointed out the inadequacy of Foucault's epistemological theories to provide for the possibility of opposition to dominant power manifestations, since "there are no relations of power without resistances."[26] But Foucault did listen to his critics and insisted that *Surveiller et punir* (*Discipline and Punish*) in 1975 was his first book in which he truly understood the importance of the body-politic.[27] He denied his ties to the structuralists from that point on, because he claimed that, whereas they analyzed forms of discourse, he was haunted by uttered and ignored discourses.[28]

Like Lacan, Foucault realized that *homo psychologicus* had to be subverted because of its false sense of integrity. Foucault had pointed out in 1961 that the modern perception of madness was "a figure made unbalanced by all that is lacking in it, by all that it conceals."[29] For Foucault, the "reasonable" systems of social justice have likewise been falsely aligned with integrity and self-sufficiency. The system by which society incarcerates "criminal" behavior perpetuates a power relationship that can only lead to its own subversion by creating a class with no political voice. And yet voices of resistance do manifest themselves among imprisoned criminals. These incarcerated voices cannot be stereotyped into oblivion as mere criminals wanting to be rejected by society. Jean Genet is an intriguing example of a person with a literary penchant to express his human malaise that has been rejected as imprisonable behavior. Foucault himself exposed other voices by directing studies published as *Un Cas de parricide* (1973, interviews of murderer Pierre Rivière), *Herculine Barbin* (1978), and Le *Désordre des familles* (1982, studies of lettres de cachet from the Bastille). With these discourses and his later studies of sexuality, power becomes less and less an institutionalized and class problem and more a question of relationships between individuals. Foucault thus moved away from a Marxist concentration on class struggle to a focus on how group dynamics had affected the individual's effort to know what was classified as unknowable.

From Georges Bataille, Foucault learned the importance of transgression for the individual confronted with institutionalized knowledge. Whereas Bataille had been writing about the repressive effects of sexual mores[30] on individuals, Foucault extended the discussion into the areas of madness, illness, and criminal imprisonment. Like Bataille, he understood the economic pressures that encouraged the efficient exclusion of nonproductive members of a society. Similarly, both of them realized that the boundaries thus introduced had to be breached in order for knowledge to be gained. Of course, for Foucault, this breach began with the "great tragic confrontation"[31] between reason and nonreason over what constituted mental illness. The "tragic" referred to the intolerant creation of asylums as symbols of the wallpapering of the differences in production generated by nonassimilated types of human behavior. Politically, the medical and legal professions were successful because society would not question the solutions of asylums for the mentally deficient, teaching clinics for the indigent sick, and prisons for criminals: these institutions were economically expedient within capitalistic systems.

The disenfranchised groups obtained an audience for their own voices in society through Foucault's sensitivity. The effect of discovering their voices is to give them power heretofore precluded by their very condition. These voices subvert the dominant choir of voices tending to homogenize people into continuous strains of ever more productive groups of people. By pointing out the discontinuities and their importance to the society itself as a humane group of intellectuals, Foucault tried to instill social responsibility for those people isolated in the margins of society and history. For this role, some called Foucault "the new Sartre."[32] In this vein, we cite Roland Barthes from 1961 as one of the early defenders of Foucault's work: "The history of madness could be 'true' only if it were naive, i.e., written by a madman, but then it could not be written in terms of history, so that we are left with the incoercible bad faith of knowledge."[33] Indeed, Foucault would lead the way in subverting the "bad faith" of what we have come to accept as "knowledge" within Western civilization.

"Ceci n'est pas une pipe"

Foucault basically intended to subvert the ideals of "knowledge" and to reveal the power of exclusion in the choices about what constitutes knowledge. In 1973, he published a study of the artist René Magritte and revealed therein the symbiotic relationship in history between the image and the text, thus interlocking discourse and visual perception as mutually reinforcing modes of knowledge. From the fifteenth to the twentieth centuries, Foucault points out, Western painting was dominated by two implied laws: either words were ruled by the image, or the image was ruled by words. Magritte's paintings broke with this traditional symbiosis and aimed to "allow discourse to collapse of its own weight and to acquire the visible shape of letters."[34] These insights transfer an idealistic or Platonic view of knowledge to a historical materialism, whereby knowledge is a means to an end.

Foucault thus shifted after 1969 or so to a "genealogy" from an "archaeology." The most important distinction between the two terms is that "genealogy" acknowledges the teleological motivation of historical materialism. As genealogy typically studies family trees in order to re-create origins and establish family succession, so Foucault's "genealogy" identified fields of study usually understood as discontinuities by traditional history. He then mapped the contiguities between those fields of study and the power relationships within traditional history that led to the exclusion of the fields of study in the margins of the history of ideas. These exclusions he called "systems of thought," the name he gave to his chair at the Collège de France in 1970.

Although Foucault had the Marxist Althusser as his professor at the École Normale Supérieure, Foucault had been very careful about identifying his historical materialism as Marxist. He respected Marx to the degree that he said: "One might even wonder what difference there could be between being a historian and being Marxist."[35] Yet he himself left the French Communist Party in 1950 and was not a Marxist thereafter. He was clearly against the domination of the ruling classes, as his studies of power and knowledge explore the subversion of this domination. But economism and the Communist prospectus were not his criteria for objecting to the hegemony of one class over another. His was a very stubborn method that sought to make sense of palimpsests in history: "Genealogy is gray, meticulous, and patiently documentary. It operates on a field of entangled and confused parchments, on documents that have been scratched over and recopied many times."[36] He was inclined toward a revisionary exploration of the ties among economics, history, and philosophy with the goal of expanding the artificial limits imposed on knowledge and society by ruling power groups.

In his genealogical orientation, Foucault revealed the roles of social institutions in the choices about what was acceptable knowledge in traditional history. Once Foucault had revealed the threats of institutionalized living, sociologists like Peter L. Berger could further investigate the consciousness of "an institutional world . . . experienced as an objective reality."[37]

One of the more pervasive studies realized by Foucault was his three-volume history of sexuality, which pointed out that the modern world "initiated sexual heterogeneities."[38] By contrast, this same world in a previous era had been driven toward industrialization and the profit motive, fostering a sexual homogenization that encouraged the bearing of children (i.e., workers among the uneducated masses) and discouraged homosexuality because it did not lead to increasing the victims of the economics of a capitalist society. Foucault's genealogy of sexuality portrayed male and female stereotypes as part of a united worldview promoting capitalist economics. Whereas his "archaeology" suggested what Georges Canguilhem (another of Foucault's former professors) hailed as "the condition of another history, in which the concept of event is preserved but in which events affect concepts and not men,"[39] Foucault's "genealogy" was to go further by presenting "the kind of disassociating view that is capable of decomposing itself, capable of shattering the unity of men's being."[40]

Foucault's presentation of human sexuality did that very thing. Since discourse plays out the human need for uniting power and knowledge, the discourse of sexuality entails another component—pleasure—in the regime of power. Foucault was very adept at separating arenas that had previously been assumed to operate as integrative spaces. He doubted that individual repression was as all-pervasive and basic as Freud and others claimed it to be. Foucault revealed the social factors in repression, especially in the ways in which discourse regulated an individual's perception of "perversions," that is, those sexual acts relegated to secrecy and not acceptable for discussion. Although "our age initiated sexual heterogeneities,"[41] the writings of Sade, Krafft-Ebing, and Bataille were historically displaced in the margins and not fit for social acceptance. The parents' bedroom was the locus for what was sexually acceptable. Nonreproductive sexual practices were under the triple edict of taboo, nonexistence, and silence.[42] This edict is ascribed to the need for the bourgeois class to gain control over its own body.

Through the sexual cultivation of the body, the bourgeois could obtain political, economic, and historical hegemony within Western society. This view is an austere portrayal of human sexuality as a paradigm of class inclusion and exclusion. As with his studies of madness, medicine, and law, the paradigm is an important lesson about knowledge derived from Foucault. Barthes's early appreciation of Foucault's writings in 1961 underscored the importance of "systems of thought": "Knowledge, whatever its conquests, its audacities, its generosities, cannot escape the relation of exclusion."[43] Whereas bourgeois economics regulated the day-to-day existence of the masses, it was the perpetuation of this economics that precluded human beings from understanding their own bodies.

The collective memory of human sexuality was being controlled. As with medical and psychological treatments as well as legal precedents, the religious confession became a key for unlocking the ties between history and existence. The discourse of Christians about their own sexuality led Foucault to understand the misery[44] within which their history had confined them. Foucault's "genealogical" discussion focused on the jurisdiction of memory to understand what is meant by historical sense: "Memory is actually a very important factor in struggle. . . . If one controls the memory of the people, one controls their dynamism. . . . It is vital to have possession of this memory, to control it, administer it, tell it what it must contain."[45] The containment of the collective memory of a people entailed establishing the limits of what could be remembered and known. Epistemological paradigms had been conceived by the Gestalt school of psychology and Thomas Kuhn among others. Foucault, however, linked epistemological paradigms to the control of society's memory and to the hegemony of economic goals.

Of course, Foucault himself was caught within bourgeois economics as a popular French writer widely read during his own lifetime. He realized that he would not be the one to free human beings from the traps of collective memory within various systems of thought. Instead, he projected to a time and place whereby human beings would exist "in a different economy of bodies and pleasure."[46] Baudrillard may indeed be announcing that new time with his work.

Foucault may not have been able to step outside his own lifetime, but like Lacan's topological sense for the unconscious, Foucault's diagram of power provided the outlines for a utopian map. This map was suggested by Gilles Deleuze who characterized Foucault's insights as conducive to a "modern topology" whereby there would be no privileged position for sources of power.[47] Instead, the privileged position is given to the vision of the cartographer, who delineates the boundaries for the battles by outlining the areas to be examined. Politically, Foucault the intellectual achieved an important social status by making a survey of the battlefield so that the strategists could plan the order of battle and deliver knowledge from the siege that social power was laying on epistemology.

The Philosopher as Cartographer

Foucault's map of the marginal areas of Western civilization has enabled us to explore areas within society heretofore thought to be asocial. Imprisonment, madness, illness, and sexual heterogeneity had been perceived as forms of social deviance prior to Foucault's insights. By cutting across the ages to study these issues, he succeeded in giving the people subject to these power struggles a place on the map of the history of knowledge. Although Richard Harland pointed out that "Foucault demonstrates for historically remote societies what Lévi-Strauss demonstrates for geographically remote societies,"[48] there is a geographical importance in Foucault's work also. He dared to carve out territories by pointing out the errors in the frontiers established as appropriate for society. He was a mapmaker who showed that the boundaries were drawn up by power brokers who relegated to the margins of society their disenfranchised victims: the imprisoned, the ill, the mental and sexual nonconformers. Although it has been said of Kuhn and his paradigms that "we cannot be assured that we are progressing over time to a more accurate picture of the world,"[49] Foucault and his paradigms bring into focus areas of the world heretofore relegated to fuzzy, obscure regions. Recalling his own comment that Magritte's paintings allow discourse "to collapse of its own weight and to acquire the visible shape of letters," Foucault's discourse reveals the struggles of power and knowledge that shore up language as a mask hiding the nefarious strategies being deployed by various hegemonies.

As with the European mapmakers of the late Middle Ages who projected the possibilities for a New World somewhere to the east, Foucault demonstrates to us today the connections between theory and practice. In his *L'Archéologie du savoir*, he had postulated that the statement (*l'énoncé*) within discourse was the key to understanding the links between power and knowledge. He then developed his role as a theorist exploring these links as he noted that theory "is a struggle against power, a struggle to reveal and undermine power where it is most invisible and insidious."[50] Although he does say that power is a struggle, he attributes power to both sides of a struggle. By doing so, Foucault dissolves the notion of dialectic as class struggle. Instead, power is a name. More specifically, Foucault claims that power is "the name that one attributes to a complex strategical situation in a particular society."[51] So he mapped out a battlefield with hazy boundaries for the new regions of intersecting politics and history.

History, however, was not terminated by Foucault. Jean Baudrillard says that history is in a state of simulation like a body in hibernation.[52] We might also take a lesson from Fernand Braudel's demonstration of the *Annales* version of history combining geography and economies to understand chronological events. Foucault's geography needs to be expanded and developed with a sensitivity to the changes involved in power struggles. The exchange of power only seems to take place because Foucault has revealed the problem areas. Baudrillard would have us understand, for example, that "power is something that is exchanged."[53] Let us look, then, to one of Foucault's teachers, Louis Althusser, for a structuralist response to how exchange takes place politically.

Chapter Six
Althusser and Antiphilosophical Philosophy

Louis Althusser was, in all likelihood, the most ironic of the five ideologists of French structuralism. He campaigned against ideology, especially the Communist version, by which the knowledge of social formations was controlled and meted out by certain protected social interests. For him, ideology was a political form of philosophy. Ironically, Althusser's incisive presentation of the dialectical and historical materialism of Karl Marx was itself an ideological discourse. Althusser was dogmatic and insistent upon the future of philosophy and science in the modern world as a result of his reading of Marx. As a member of the Communist Party from 1948 until his death, he ignored critiques that his Marxism was elitist and untimely (he did not predict the May 1968 student revolts nor did he advocate uniting the students and the workers' causes at that time); insensitive to the political realities of national boundaries (he did not object to the Soviet invasion of Czechoslovakia in 1968); and participating in the threats of political hegemony (he refused to jettison Stalin's system of Marxism when it became clear that personal control had transformed Soviet Marxism into a totalitarian nightmare).

This blindness to the political realities of his time made Althusser an embarrassment to some of his colleagues. Foucault did not acknowledge him as his professor nor as the immediate source for the term "epistemological break," so crucial to Foucault's own paradigms. A cartoon by Maurice Henry, mentioned in the first chapter, illustrates the disappearing act performed on Althusser by those who remembered his historical faux pas. In the cartoon Foucault is holding forth in a very lively manner to his structuralist peers. But Althusser is not present. It is as if Foucault's presence was a palimpsest for Althusser's teachings. And yet Althusser had a strong following in the early 1960s and was influential in the French "new philosophy" of the 1970s.

Louis Althusser was a voice crying within the French Communist Party for a special kind of Marxian reading he called "symptomatic" of the unconscious dimensions in Marx's writings. "Marxian" is an adjective to describe what is characteristic of Marx himself by contrast with what his disciples have made of him ("Marxist"). He laid claim to being what Edith Kurzweil called "a superreader" of Marx.[1] He could see that most bourgeois readers were blind to the real Marx because they had superimposed their bourgeois values on a literal reading of Marx's early writings, wherein a Hegel-inspired Marx promoted economism, technocratism, and humanism. All three were bourgeois readings that oversimplified Marx, according to Althusser. These readings did not recognize a "break" in Marx's thinking around 1845, when he appeared to have become scientifically oriented. This moment, according to Althusser, represented an "epistemological break" in Marx's writings and warranted a "symptomatic" reading sensitive to the maturing of the holistic theory of Karl Marx.

Thus Althusser revealed the "myth of a Hegelian Marx" who had simply inverted Hegel's dialectic into a materialist one. Althusser personally assumed the mission to demythologize this Marx with a philosophy all too sure of itself. He advocated a "symptomatic reading" (*une lecture symptômale*) of Marx that would reveal the mature writings of Marx as the true Marxian message for the modern world. I shall discuss the components of that message, which was severely criticized by Althusser's peers for its lack of congruency with the early writings of Marx as well as with Marx's *Grundrisse* (Outlines). Despite these critiques, his political insensitivities, and his inconsistencies in claiming to be Marxist and/or structuralist, Althusser's influence has been substantial, to the extent that he has been identified as "the main theorist of structuralist causality."[2]

It is ironic that Althusser called Lacan "a magnificent pathetic Harlequin,"[3] because Althusser himself became the French Communist clown accusing non-Marxist structuralists and nonstructuralist Marxists alike of being unscientific. He espoused a "scientific" version of Marx in contradistinction to the "ideological" Marx constructed by bourgeois readers. For Althusser, "ideology" was philosophical as a weltanschauung with assumptions about values and systems of meanings. And yet his training as a philosopher stayed with him, as his reading of the mature, scientific Marx was itself an "ideology." This ideology was a structuralist one, from which Foucault separated himself and which borrowed from the intellectual developments of Lévi-Strauss and Lacan. On the one hand, Foucault was careful not to identify himself as Althusser's pupil even though Althusser and Georges Canguilhem were, significantly, his teachers at the École Normale Supérieure. It was Althusser who reminded his readers that Foucault "was a pupil of mine."[4] Meanwhile, Foucault would deny being a Marxist or a structuralist, as his "genealogical" method gave teleological motivation to historical materialism and dissolved the dialectic by attributing power to both sides of social struggles.

On the other hand, three other major ideologists of French structuralism had overlapping influences on Althusser. Whereas the anti-Sartrean tone of Althusser's early Marxist essays is similar to the Barthes of *Le Degré zéro de l'écriture*, Althusser specifically reacted to the anthropological myth of *Homo Oeconomicus* popularized by Lévi-Strauss in his adaptations of the Marcel Mauss theories of gifts and potlatch. This myth illustrated that individuals had clearly defined economic needs and demands that regulated the social, cultural, and political dimensions of their existence. Thirdly, Althusser applied Lacan's views of the originating subject and law as well as the psychoanalytic concepts of "overdetermination" and "symptomatic reading" in reacting to the overly bourgeois assessments of the writings of Karl Marx. Overdetermination was a Freudian term for a single dream image expressing several unconscious desires. This concept, when linked with the symptomatic reading method for meanings beneath the surface, led to Althusser's arguments for structuralist causality: the *Darstellung*. This German word, used by Marx, meant "representation" and referred to the act of understanding a structure only as a whole.

Althusser thus distinguished himself from the other French structuralists by a view of causality that would replace an outworn view of history. I shall now discuss that history, the "epistemological break" that brought a new awareness, class struggle revealed as the key to historical understanding, the new science of history, and finally, the new philosophy revealed by Althusser in his reading of Karl Marx.

History without Subject or Goal(s)

As with the other ideologists of French structuralism, the question of history, as the keeper of causality, is paramount in Althusser's view of things. Althusser looked back at Marx's writings to retrieve a nonidealistic and nonbourgeois sense of history. Marx had critiqued Hegel to reveal the myth of the originating subject, a belief that reflection allows humanity to see itself within a setting of time and space. Marx had pointed out, however, that the human mind was the primary driving force behind causality and that causality was an invention of a thinking subject too sure of its powers to originate social linkages. In addition, Althusser noted that "ideology" is problematic for history in influencing how individuals read events and then construct the apparent links generally identified as causality. This "ideology" is "a system (with its own logic and rigor) of representations (images, myths, and ideas depending on the situation) gifted with a historic existence and role at the heart of a given society."[5] Such an "ideology" also precedes the founding of any science for Althusser and becomes political philosophy that structures readings before they take place, because history and historical time are ideological concepts.[6] Ideology assigns arbitrary causal significance to the links within history. Therefore, there are no "innocent" readings of the causal structures of history.

This same explanation of "ideology" can be helpful in understanding the five major players in French structuralism, because all five, including Althusser, who never saw himself in this light, became "ideologists" as they each adopted their own individualized method for structuralist thinking and had their own historical influence on others who developed and expanded on these methods. Of course, all five also influenced each other's methods as they were popularly linked together as "structuralists."

Nevertheless, Althusser learned from his readings of Marx that there were spatial rather than causal structures in history. While Lévi-Strauss relied too much on a "chance" view of history that could not distinguish between different and successive social formations,[7] Althusser advocated Marxian historical materialism as the science of history because it is rooted in the struggles of social formations and can distinguish historical events by their effects. This "new" form of history invented by Marx as a science could also preclude "Stalin's ideological pair,"[8] humanism and economism from Marxist history. Althusser did realize the oppression in Stalin's regime. For Althusser, however, the oppression was mainly ideological. Stalin had conceived of language as an overarching superstructure and controlled it with his ideals of humanism and economism. Althusser noted Stalin's fascination with superstructures and attributed political oppression within his regime to his enchantment with the overriding linguistic formulas of humanism and economism.

This Stalinist ideological pairing of humanism and economism was an idealistic projection of social reality, according to Althusser. On the one hand, humanism would have social formations begin in the theoretical formations and projections of the human mind as an originating subject. In *Pour Marx* (1965), Althusser presented Marx as antihumanist in the proposal for historical materialism, rooted as it was in class struggle. As opposed to originating subjects guiding the idealistic superstructure of humanism, members of society were understood by the mature Marx as "supports" (*Trager*)[9] for the modes of production.

In adapting this portrayal of the individual, Althusser's antihumanist reading engendered a particularly poignant debate with the British Communist John Lewis, who had promoted the links among ethics, morality, and

Communism in a Feuerbach-like spirit. Socialist humanists like Lewis accused Althusser of being out of touch with the early Hegelian, humanistic Marx. Althusser's reply (*Réponse à John Lewis*, 1973) recapitulated his various positions by citing the "later" (i.e., after 1845) Marx and Lenin as his major sources for a new political science incorporating historical materialism ("new history") and dialectical materialism ("new philosophy") to replace the falsifying ideology of a humanistic Marx.

Economism was another idealistic superstructure that falsified history. Basically, this was a bourgeois reading of Marx, whereby the *Homo Oeconomicus*,[10] another idealist portrayal of humanity rendered fashionable by the anthropological myths narrated by Lévi-Strauss, supporting a political economy arbitrarily residing outside history, reduced the understanding of social formations to a linear, mechanical causality in a homogeneous space. That homogeneous space was a bourgeois world whereby Marx was reduced to an economic savior because, as a reaction to the Twentieth International Communist Congress in 1956 when Stalin's purges were exposed, many Marxists began to reread the Hegelian writings of the young Marx, especially the *Economic and Philosophic Manuscripts of 1844*. As Hegel preferred a reading whereby "the true kernel was retrieved from the mystified shell," so Marx was chiefly appreciated for his pronouncements on such issues as money, private property, and labor as the tools of political economy. Althusser objected to the appropriation of an "essential" Marx from writings that evolved toward a historical vision wherein science and philosophy could be reconciled in the theory of social formation.

Two philosophers, Jacques Martin and Gaston Bachelard, contributed key concepts to the Althusserian reading of Marx. On the one hand, Martin conceived of the term "problematic" to express the "unity of a theoretical formulation."[11] The term was used throughout Althusser's writings to express clusters of ideas, heretofore considered independent of each other. On the other hand, Gaston Bachelard was a trained mathematician and professor of physics who became a philosopher of science and in that latter capacity was Althusser's advisor for a thesis at the École Normale Supérieure entitled "The Notion of Content in Hegel's Philosophy." Bachelard conceived of the phrase "epistemological break" (*coupure épistémologique*) to speak of the mutation from a prescientific to a scientific way of thinking.

Georges Canguilhem, another of Althusser's instructors at the École Normale, also encouraged Althusser's use of the concept "epistemological break" as a way to understand history. Generally, Bachelard thought that philosophy came to the service of science after the founding of the science. But prior to the invention of a science, certain evidence of the senses and primary truths of consciousness could no longer be trusted. The world "problematic" could be used to identify these prescientific beliefs. Althusser identified this problematic as an ideological one with reference to Marx, who discovered for himself in about 1845 the importance of science for the theory of social formation. Likewise, during the early 1960s, Althusser developed the problematic of the mature Marx, who had discovered the possibilities of a "new science" to expose the spatial structures of class struggle. Although Henri Lefebvre tried to unite Marxism and structuralism in 1968 by speaking of "a certain coherence"[12] within Marxian thought, Althusser had already succeeded by then in popularizing the "epistemological break" in Marx, thus creating a lacunary Marx with two separate identities to be confronted by modern Marxism.

Marx's Epistemological Break

The French structuralists have in common a fascination with exploring the depths to counter their distrust of appearances. So it was with Althusser. His disdain for the bourgeois Marxism of his time (despite the fact that Marx himself began from a bourgeois perspective) led him to question a superficial reading of Marx and thereby to discover a kindred spirit in Marx.

In *Capital*, Althusser had found Marx on the verge of discovering the value of science, to the disparagement of Hegel's phenomenological humanism: "If the essences were not different from the phenomena, if the essential interior was not different from the inessential or phenomenal exterior, there would be no need for science."[13] This observation by Marx was crucial for Althusser, because it aligned Althusser's structuralist vision of spatial structures in history with Marx's perspective of science revealing the *Darstellung* or "representation" of social formation in history. By studying the effects of a social structure, Marx had intuited a scientific model for a "new history" and had concomitantly rejected his previous Hegelian-inspired "error to think that philosophy is a science."[14] Althusser pointed out that this moment was not, as many Hegelian readers of Marx interpret it, a simple inversion by Marx of the Hegelian dialectic because, in Althusser's words, "a science is not obtained by simply inverting an ideology."[15] Bachelard's insights into the inception of a new science by means of an epistemological break gave Althusser the perspective to present the differences between the ideological Marx and the scientific Marx by explaining Marx's new science as a rupture from worn philosophical views of social formation.

The ideal of humanism, for example, assumed an originating subject for reflection on philosophical questions. But Marx's discovery of science gave him the insight that political entities are "supports" (*Trager*) and in this role cannot originate reflection. Instead, the "masses" make history as they are involved in "class struggle." It has been noted that Althusser did not examine what Marx meant by "masses" or "classes,"[16] so it is difficult to be precise in adapting Althusser's model to study a particular social formation. Nevertheless, Althusser portrayed the epistemological break in Marx as a turning away from the individual in society toward the political struggles of groups with each other. The ideological implications of humanism were too restrictive, as Marx envisioned a "new science" with its accompanying "new philosophy" as capable of studying the class struggles in historical and dialectical materialism. The Hegelian dialectic, with its focus on the idea as the principle overriding its totality, was too concerned with essences for Marx. So Marx had to dissociate himself from Hegel, Fichte, and Feuerbach, who were all impassioned by essentialist humanism.

The identity of the "new science" proposed by Marx is debatable. Some would have it be economics. This is the naive "economism" rejected by Althusser as too bourgeois. Others portray it as technology, this being the simplistic reading of Marx that Althusser called "technocratism." For his part, Althusser projected the "new science" as history capable of understanding the spatial, rather than the causal or temporal, structures of social configuration. In its antihumanistic posture, such a "history" would preclude the phenomenological self-questioning of reflection, because "the tendency of Marx's scientific work is to relieve him of the philosophical categories in question."[17] The break was clean in that the "new science" left the "old philosophy" or ideology behind and set up the parameters for its own, "new" philosophy. The new science created its own space by having its own agenda in terms of the materialist, rather than essentialist (i.e., Hegelian), focus on the effects of a given social formation.

In Althusser's debate with John Lewis about the antihumanistic sense of Marx, Althusser went to great lengths to distinguish science from philosophy. He called traditional philosophy "politics in theory," that is, ideology, to distinguish this study from the "new philosophy," which was to be much more closely aligned with Marx's new science by providing parameters, methodological guidance, mathematical verification, and theory. The inspiration for Althusser here is Spinoza—the seventeenth-century philosopher whose ethical thought so involved science, mathematics, and philosophy that he was condemned by his peers, ideologically aligned with either Judaism or the Church. Althusser admired the intellectual rigor of Spinoza and saw the mature Marx of *Capital* so inspired: "The truth of his theorem is a hundred per cent provided by criteria purely internal to the practice of mathematical proof."[18] Mathematics provided a model for the theoretical practice of Marx's new science. Althusser understood that whereas science articulated propositions that were demonstrations, it was philosophy's task to provide the theses to be examined. One of these theses was at the base of the Marxian view of social configuration: that class struggle is the basis for all political existence.

The Driving Force of History

Althusser claimed that humanism precludes people from realizing that class struggle is the motor of social existence. By promoting the good of the individual and the power of the originating subject, humanism could not properly be allied with the central doctrine of Marxism: class struggle. Social classes do not always already exist in society. Rather, the word *struggle* is crucial, because classes are only the result of the social contests to organize and differentiate in groups. For Althusser's Marx, class struggle is the social enactment of the primacy of contradiction in social formation. That is, the individual joins a class to attain personal power in a collective identity and at the same time goes through self-effacement as the class interests predominate in the historical achievements of that class. People organize themselves into unions, political parties, and other units in order to demonstrate their power as a group. The struggles to attain, maintain, and overthrow these social groups invigorate society and give structure to each society, but these are spatial structures in that their makeup is based on struggling relationships.

By studying the nature of this struggle, one understands what Althusser called "the myth of origins,"[19] whereby the human subject or individual is assumed to be in control of historical events. So history must be reconceived to place the class struggle in its Marxian-Leninist portrayal as "the motor of history." According to Althusser, this activity of the social struggle for class differentiation was the focus for Marx's new science as well as for an ensuing new philosophy.

Althusser generated considerable opposition to his statement that philosophy is "the struggle of the classes in theory." Generally, Althusser meant that it was philosophy's task to provide a theoretical framework for understanding class struggle. But despite his silence during the Soviet invasion of Czechoslovakia in 1968, he would later try to identify the political problem as one posed by the Czechs: "What the Czechs wanted was socialism within a national independence and not humanism."[20] Althusser's critics came down hard on him for his refusal to become involved earlier and saw his thesis of philosophy as class struggle in theory as, typically, "an alibi for political immobilism."[21] Ironically, once again, despite Althusser's claim to be studying struggle and class structure in formation, his perspective was identified, by E. P. Thompson, as a static structuralism in that he did not discuss the dialogue between social being and social consciousness.[22] So, for example, Stalinism, fascism, racism, or the affluence of the contemporary working class were not discussed as within the context of class struggle by Althusser. In defense of Althusser, however, it should be noted, as Raymond Aron pointed out,[23] that Althusser did not make claims to provoke political commitments for or against systems of thought. He was always already a Communist and merely wrote his books to justify his attitudes. He was much more a political philosopher than a political activist, which he never claimed to be.

Althusser did claim that Marxism should not be Hegelian politics. And yet, in his own way, Althusser himself was Hegelian by promoting class struggle as the principal idea governing Marx's dialectical materialism without the involvement in daily political reality that characterized the dialectic as materialist. Once again, Thompson, who has proven to be the most thorough of Althusser's critics while defending his own turf as a historian, provided an apt phrase to describe Althusser's intent in placing the class struggle at the heart of philosophy: "the orrery of system."[24] An "orrery" is a mechanical model of the solar system, and Althusser's model was a bit too mechanical in its presentation of class struggle. Like Lévi-Strauss, the system became theoretical hegemony and precluded many details. Perhaps system was synonymous for him with the method of the new science. Let us see then how he portrayed the new Marxian science that focused on the grounding of social formation on class struggle.

Historical Materialism as a Science

Althusser told us that historical materialism was one of the two new perspectives unveiled by Marx's discovery of the importance of science. Historical materialism was Marx's term for history. The materialism was his contribution to the history of ideas. Marx studied the effects of social formation and thereby focused on the material of history. Althusser insisted that this was the "new science" built on the "theoretical anti-humanism"[25] of Marx to provide a structuralist model of history. We recall that Marx viewed individuals as *Trager*, that is, as functionaries or supports for the class struggle, rather than the active agents in history within a humanist explanation. Althusser then went a step further to compose a history text for Marx: "The text of history is not a text in which a voice (the Logos) speaks, but the inaudible and illegible notation of the effects of a structure of structures."[26] This "structure of structures" is Althusser's contribution to French structuralism by providing a theory of structuralist causality.

The "structure of structures" has two principal characteristics: its depiction and its manifestation. First of all, Althusser's Marx used the German word *Darstellung* (representation) to signify the whole of which any structure is a part. For example, if the class struggle of Fascism in Italy in the 1930s is studied, the larger structure of the Church and its influence on Italian cultural values must be admitted as a whole from which a part is taken to be examined. In effect, the whole makes visible the underground network of support (class members as *Träger*) for what appears to be an obvious social formation. Since representation is so crucial to the way structuralists in general probe appearances to find a gold mine lurking beneath unreliable surface clutter, André Glucksmann, one of the French "new philosophers," understands *Darstellung* as "the key to Althusserian structuralism."[27]

It could also be said that "overdetermination" is an equally important key to unlocking the "structure of structures." The term was taken from Freud, who used it to express the way in which a single dream-image incorporates several unconscious desires. Althusser adapted the term to explain the manifestation in class struggles of economic, political, and ideological forces that develop unevenly and yet provide a balance of influences on a given class struggle to achieve a certain effect. These forces come together in a "conjuncture" of influences. Althusser especially angered his peers by using overdetermination to explain Stalinism and the Chinese Cultural Revolution, allowing ideology to have relative autonomy in those historical contexts, despite his own insistence that Marx would have the new science replace the unreliable truths of the link between ideology and empiricism. This inconsistency on Althusser's part demonstrated his own "blind Marxist faith after all."[28]

Ironically again, Spinoza's *experientia vaga*, experience as the medium of illusion, was an inspiration to Althusser as he explained Marx's historical materialism. The "structure of structures" was to be grounded in the human experiences of class struggle. But Althusser produced something different from the rigorous mathematical model for science and philosophy proposed by Spinoza.

Historical research, however, was not Althusser's strength. Since his reflections on class struggle were too marked by what André Glucksmann called a "metaphysical passion for system,"[29] Althusser's application of the new science of history was doomed to be too disconnected from experience. In his debate with John Lewis, he did acknowledge Lewis's reservation about the science advocated by Althusser's Marx, that is, that Marx's new science should include all the social sciences and not be naively understood as the natural or physical sciences so driven by empiricism. Nevertheless, Althusser never came to terms with the application of this new science with historical experiences. One explanation is that Althusser was so insistent in his anti-humanism, in his claim that individuals have not made history but were simply vectors driven by an ulterior structural determinism (the class struggle and ideological overdetermination), that he would not understand either Lenin or Stalin as controlling the political system with personal visions of hegemony. Althusser himself was also justifying his own dogmatism by seeing himself merely as an elucidator of the real Marx. And yet, as Piaget expressed it, the ethereal Marx who emerges "has too low an estimate of things human."[30] Neither historians nor Marxists could accept Althusser's theory of Marx as soundly grounded in their disciplines. And yet the fact that they paid attention to Althusser at all is a commentary on their nervousness about the revolutionary implications of his "symptomatic reading" of Marx.

Despite Althusser's shortcomings, his work does warrant serious investigation. As an idealist, his theory of Marx the Scientist spawned a whole generation of thinkers in the 1970s concerned with the other side of the double-edged sword that was Marx's epistemological break: new philosophy. After all, Althusser was trained as a philosopher and yearned for a political philosophy that was not subject to ideology.

Toward a New Philosophy

In his association with French structuralism, Althusser paved the way for the eventual demise and replacement of the study of structures with a concern for communication. His own lack of communication with historical events such as the May 1968 student and worker revolts or Stalinism was an example of the asocial abstractions that could be spawned by structuralist reflection. Although he denied in 1965 that philosophy was the "theory of theoretical practice"[31] and then restored the priority of politics over theory in 1969, as late as 1979 his critics accused him of "remaining somewhat static"[32] in his structuralist posture. He was not discussing the relationships among the structures so much as the structures of social formation. As another of his Marxist contemporaries, Henri Lefebvre, noted, for Marx himself "the transitions are more profound, more real, and truer than the structures."[33] The struggle is paramount, rather than the class or the form of the class, because work is the heart of dialectical materialism, the philosophy created by Marx as he sought to define the parameters of his new science.

One of the dangers of an unchecked faith in science is that it could lead to a technocratic separation of knowledge from social welfare. As I shall discuss in the next chapter, there have been vigorous reactions to the Althusserian proposal of linking Marxism with science. For example, Jürgen Habermas of the second-generation Frankfurt School is developing a view of Marx as a hagiographer of work to the exclusion of thought, such that philosophy must save the world from a technocracy by reuniting knowledge with human interests. Meanwhile, the struggle of thinking was the focus of Marx's new philosophy of dialectical materialism, according to Althusser, because "a real theoretical practice . . . produces knowledge."[34]

Althusser's reading of Marx entailed a new philosophy capable of guiding the new science. As the new science would begin revealing different relationships or structures as a result of its work, then the accumulation of these structures could also lead to contradictions without a voice to speak about what is being discovered and how the discoveries are linked to each other. In fact, the contradictions would be there in any case. The new philosophy assumes in its agenda the task of pointing out the contradictions so that the new science can continue to explore dominant structures that may not appear as central or major at first glance. Althusser's "symptomatic reading," however, borrowed from the psychoanalytic explorations by Lacan, could reveal the unconscious text of appearances as his theory claims to be. Just as Althusser claimed that such a reading of *Capital* would lead to a discovery of the closed circle of Marx's experience, so new philosophy can explore the logic of new science to expose the limits as well as discuss the contradictions and gaps in the theoretical unity of this logic.

In ironic contrast to Foucault's introductory lecture to the Collège de France called *L'Ordre du discours*, Althusser's elitist university Marxism was called "a discourse of order" (*un discours de l'ordre*).[35] This term was used by one of Althusser's disenchanted, former students, Jacques Rancière, to speak of the logical hypotheses offered by new philosophy that could not deal with the disorder of worker revolts or student uprisings (these individuals were called "progressivists" by Althusser), as opposed to Foucault who worked with experiences and thereby proposed hypotheses about society and its real people (the insane, the sick, the sexually deviant) conveniently hidden by society. And yet Althusser's voice was involved in the political reality of the French Communist Party. Despite Rancière's objection about the order of Althusser's Marx, Althusser criticized, in a pamphlet against the French form of Marxism, the "language of amalgamation"[36] whereby Georges Marchais of the French Communist newspaper *L'Humanité* spoke of the unity of the PCF in the Twenty-Second International but ignored the debates about the disparity between the workers and the Marxist theories of the PCF, thus effectively silencing the "appeal rising from the militants and the masses."[37] This

pamphlet by Althusser showed him to be still committed to the class struggle, after so many of his peers had criticized him for being too abstract with
his theory.

There is something admirable in Althusser's insistence that philosophy
does have social responsibility. The French tradition of such involvement in
the modern era includes Émile Zola (the Dreyfus Affair); Julien Benda (*La
Trahison des clercs*, 1927); Jean-Paul Sartre (his life, e.g., the Manifesto of
the 121 against the Algerian War); and Raymond Aron (see his *Mémoires* for
the struggle of being Jewish, Marxist, and intellectual in France from the
1930s to the 1970s), among many others. And Althusser, the structuralist
and Marxist, gave the social responsibility of philosophy another dimension
by providing the impetus for the discussion of a political epistemology and
the organization of the French "new philosophers" in the 1970s.

Chapter Seven
Alternate Sciences of Politics

The ironies in Louis Althusser's program for a Marxist structuralism point toward the contradictions in both Marxism and French structuralism. The five major ideologists were not able to provide viable political means to realize their "revolutionary" goals for looking at history in a synchronic fashion. Althusser came the closest to a political vision with his symptomatic reading of Marx. But he fell short because he was not able to link Marx's prospectus for a new science and a new philosophy with the contemporary politics and history of the 1960s.

The year 1968 brought some key events. Although Charles de Gaulle was called the first structuralist chief of state, it was precisely his own preoccupation with the glory of France and his lack of historical connection with the causes of the students and workers that led to his political demise. His command of language had a rhetorical flair that transcended the historical moment and finally proved not to be connected with it. Althusser's method of using a symptomatic reading would have indeed been useful to reveal the political intersections of ideology, philosophy, and science in de Gaulle's language.

Nevertheless, the French Marxism of the PCF was not politically viable as Althusser presented it. Indeed, he was correct to point out that "the simple only ever exists in a complex structure."[1] His model of the "complex structure" did not connect well enough with the political reality of his historical moment. Curiously enough, Marx had provided a warning in his *Theses on Feuerbach,* which had been ignored by Althusser as being too "Hegelian": the true intellectual wealth of the individual depends entirely on real relationships."[2] Althusser's own credibility was undermined by his lack of these "real relationships." And yet his work was important for other structuralist ventures that it spawned. Although the word *structuralist* became less popular in the years following 1968, important French writers nevertheless continued the causes of the ideologists by expanding the political, ideological, and scientific networking of the examination of language. Foucault, in his preface to the English translation of *L'Anti-Oedipe* by Gilles Deleuze and Félix Guattari, pointed to this expansionist exercise with caveats suggested by their work: "Do not use thought to ground a political practice in truth; nor political action to discredit, as mere speculation, a line of thought. Use political practice as an intensifier of thought."[3] Such a melding of politics and intellectual leadership was a laudable goal as France turned away from the insurrections of May 1968 and headed into the 1970s.

The problematic of the ideologists of French structuralism was largely contained within the ironies of Althusser's work. The reason is that he was connected in so many ways to the four others. The Althusserian problematic sets the stage for the French "New Philosophers" who appeared in direct reaction to Althusser's failed Marxism. Philosophy and science would come together in the heritage of Gaston Bachelard, who as a scientist and philosopher claimed that the history of science had been radically changed by modern calculus. Although Bachelard died in 1962, his work bred a whole generation of scholars continuing his prospectus for a non-Cartesian "new scientific spirit" (the title of one of his monographs published in 1934). His most gifted students continuing in the French structuralist tradition were Gilles Deleuze (b. 1925) and Michel Serres (b. 1930). Both wrote books about Spinoza. And both offered alternatives to Lacan's psychoanalysis. Deleuze (with Guattari, a Lacanian psychoanalyst) called his alternative schizoanalysis. Basically, the method entails looking at differences as the key to a new scientific spirit. The "series" is offered as an alternative to structure by allowing insertion, disequilibrium, shapelessness, and perpetuity. Meanwhile, Serres proposed a mathematically inspired method called logo-analysis that focused on communication rather than on the immobile, ordered form of linguistic structure.

Serres and Deleuze were thus able to begin moving French structuralist thought into a politically viable mode. Their antistructuralist structures would enable the French to rethink history and how dominant ideologies had imposed fixed notions about what political involvement meant. In this chapter, I shall examine the increasing need of French intellectuals to break out of the structuralist program in order to become more politically astute with their scientific programs.

The Ironies of Althusser

Althusser insisted on the spurious nature of the originating subject, and yet his readings of Marx are teleological. He did not see the contradictions between what he was saying and what he was doing. Today those contradictions help us to see why French structuralism was not politically viable. The disparity between the ahistorical positions of the structuralist ideologists and the political reality of France in the late 1960s was too great to be ignored. In 1961, Althusser had challenged Sartre's existential prospectus in a debate at the École Normale Supérieure in Paris with the observation that "the Sartrean *cogito* was difficult to maintain within a Marxist conception of History."[4] And by 1968, it was the Marxist conception of history, as narrated by Althusser, that dissolved as the students and workers saw Sartre on the barricades in the streets of Paris. And yet the structuralists spoke about the political implications of the "structure" in ways that promised more than they delivered. Lévi-Strauss, for example, noted in his *Tristes Tropiques* in 1955: "The structure of the village does something more than make possible the refined working of the institution. It both sums up and insures the relationships between man and the universe, society and the supernatural world, and between the living and the dead."[5]

The ideology implicit in the programs offered by the French structuralists reflected where society had been rather than where it should go. Lévi-Strauss, Barthes, Lacan, Foucault, and Althusser all offered testimony to the "death of man" as humanism had promoted man to be—an ethnocentric, originating subject in control of the forces of history.[6] All five succeeded as "master thinkers" within the French university system, either in the Collège de France or at the École Normale Supérieure. The term "master thinkers" was the title of a book by André Glucksmann, one of the leading French "new philosophers" in the early 1970s. Glucksmann was perceptive in noting the links between state institutions and the promotion of ideologies by "master thinkers": "It is easy to see that the lever of ideology has a fulcrum: the power of the state. All ideologies channel through the state the transformation of the world that they plan to effect. The master thinkers were the fathers of the reigning ideologies, in that they provided the state with their reasons of state."[7] Although Althusser had complained that an ideological Marx was dominating Marxist thought, Althusser's own teleology for a scientifically oriented Marx substituted one ideology for another within the École Normale and, he hoped, within the French PCF.

All this struggle about the "true Marx" did bring a certain awareness to the workers and the students that ran counter to Althusser's promotion of Marx within France's state institutions. Appropriately, Deleuze remarked that, in the wake of all the controversy about Marx, what ensued was "as if a complicity about the state were finally broken."[8] Ideology would be working, rather than reflective. Althusser's philosophy had been too abstract. As some of his Belgian disciples recently maintained, his proposal that philosophy be the theoretical class struggle had a twofold purpose: (1) to carry on the class struggle on a philosophical level, and (2) to bring to intellectuals the intensity of the social struggle.[9] His proposal, however, was not grounded in the work of society.

For Althusser, the work to be accomplished was an epistemology distinct from the physical struggles of the classes. And so, the Cartesian spirit of the body-mind dichotomy characterized the work of the French structuralists as exemplified by Lévi-Strauss in his search for the "human spirit," Barthes in his early flirtations with semiology and a "science of literature," Lacan in his tripartite examination of the psyche, and Foucault with his épistemès.

The May 1968 uprisings, however, did bring about some changes in their work. Barthes published his *Roland Barthes pa Roland Barthes,* which is a great testimony to the admixture of his thinking body. Foucault shifted from epistemological concerns with his archaeological method to social interests in power, position, and alienation. And Lacan became more emphatic in his rejection of the originating subject. Epistemology was incapable of explaining social change. Knowledge had to be integrated with physical work.

Alternatives to Descartes were being studied for models linking the whole person to knowledge and social change. Since the energizing effect of work made thermodynamics an especially appealing model for studying structures linking knowledge and social action, Pierre Gassendi, a seventeenth-century contemporary of Descartes, was attractive for his slogan *ambulo ergo sum*—I walk, therefore I am—the motto for his claim that thermodynamics was the principle of life itself.[10] Spinoza, as a seventeenth-century successor to Descartes, also offered an alternative to the Cartesian separation of body and mind with his ethical monism. In addition, Jean-Marie Benoist, in his *La Révolution structuraliste* (1975), cited Leibnitz as the philosophical forerunner of Bachelard and Michel Serres in presenting a philosophy of harmony with his monads. And, of course, Heidegger's *Being and Time* (1927) was reread for its philosophical arguments about grounding existence in being rather than in knowledge (the mind) or physical work (the body).

With all these alternatives to Descartes being read and discussed, Michel Serres was thus moved to propose a "pluralist epistemology"[11] that would be capable of accounting for the interconnections among knowledge, the world, and human intersubjectivity (*la cité humaine*). He claimed that this prospectus would provide a "reinvigorated scientific spirit."[12]

These speculations were still "structuralist" because they were based on a search for structures within language. Even after 1968, language continued to attract researchers in a common forum. Perhaps the reason was the failure of writers like the five ideologists, who were all very popular in academic and intellectual circles in Paris and yet all were unable to prepare French society for the political fiasco of May 1968. André Martinet had spoken in the early

1960s about the phenomenon of "double articulation,"[13] whereby language could be analysed on two planes, on the level of phonic form and on the level of meaning. And there was the rub, because all the exercises in dialectical thinking by the French structuralists were not necessarily perceived as such when exemplified in a language determined differently by its readers. Similarly, Émile Benveniste had commented on the doubling effect of phenomena perceived as data by the French structuralists: "The phenomena belonging to the interhuman milieu . . . have the characteristic that they can never be taken as simple data or defined in the order of their own nature but must always be understood as double from the fact that they are connected to something else."[14] Both of these respected structural linguists, Martinet and Benveniste, identified the problems. Yet the five ideologists did not expound on serious political positions for the structures they discovered. So the French New Philosophers represented a new generation by sketching a politics that was missing within Althusser's grand plan for a Marxian political philosophy.

The New Philosophers and the Master Thinkers

Some of Althusser's disenchanted students left his following to prepare their own politically sensitive vision for a "new philosophy" rising out of Marx's appreciation for the role of science within the class struggle. The principal writers involved were Bernard-Henri Lévy, André Glucksmann, Christian Jambet, Guy Lardreau, Philippe Nemo, and Maurice Clavel.

Glucksmann's *Les Maîtres Penseurs* (*The Master Thinkers*) set the anti-totalitarian tone of the group as they explored ways to continue their own political activism in May 1968. Glucksmann was influenced by Aleksandr Solzhenitsyn's portrayal of Soviet oppression since 1918 to question the hegemony with which Western intelligentsia hand over their power only to other intelligentsia. Glucksmann's agenda was not to reject Marx out of hand and to lean toward the right politically, as he and the other "new philosophers" were incorrectly portrayed. Instead, he did point out that Marxism was too facile in its vision by providing "not one word so far about the archipelagoes of our history."[15] "Archipelagoes," of course, is a reference to Solzhenitsyn's *The Gulag Archipelago* and decries the isolationist positions of Marxists who insist on interpreting Marx within the cadre of three other major thinkers: Fichte, Hegel, and Nietzsche. Marx is not rejected out of hand, however. It is Marx who, according to Glucksmann, "offers a strategic grid for deciphering, and so for organizing, the major conflicts of the modern world."[16] The problem was how Marxism related, or didn't relate, to "our history."

The issue of social responsibility on the part of intellectuals returned in the debates generated by the New Philosophers. Bernard-Henri Lévy led populist rallies for the New Philosophers, who were outraged when the Vincennes campus of the University of Paris was bulldozed in the summer of 1980. That campus had been built as an institutional reaction to the May 1968 student revolts. Its destruction was symbolic of a wallpapering of history, of a false sense of freedom from the hegemonic voices within the French Academy. Jambet and Lardreau had warned society that "the discourse of liberation, by introducing desire as an entirely false vision and by having the master be misunderstood, assumes the same role."[17] Instead, they proposed an "angelic discourse," whereby intellectuals would become guides to human power disguised by various political and/or ideological masks.[18]

The New Philosophers thus sought ways to preclude Althusser's overdetermination of class struggle. As Jean-Paul Sartre and Raymond Aron overreacted to the May 1968 events by encouraging all intellectuals to link together Marxism with social causes, Lévy charged that intellectuals had a greater responsibility to society in providing the vision of clear, independent thinking. In his *Éloge des intellectuels* (Eulogy for the intellectuals) in 1987, he encouraged intellectuals to realize that there is also a "terrorism of involvement" whereby reality is reduced to a single "-ism" or way of looking at social problems. Likewise, Maurice Clavel called for the disenchanted Leftists from the 1960s, frustrated by not having transformed French culture, to join the cause of the New Philosophers by being vigilant in questioning the reforms in education and in working conditions advocated by pseudo-Marxist groups.[19] Lévy even asserted that Marx was becoming the Machiavelli of this century in providing a handbook about how to rule.[20] Socialists and those who claimed to be Marxian had to be vigilant that the government was not disguising hegemony with a pseudoliberal political label.

Political responsibility became an abiding theme for the New Philosophers. Structures of memory were equally important, as both Glucksmann and Lévy invoked the Holocaust and the example of Hitler's Germany to remind their peers of the threats of hegemony. Deleuze pointed to Foucault's presentation of memory as a doubling or folding effect whereby some events are tucked away in the creases created by the very activity of doubling selected acts.[21] The word *fold,* as a metaphor for human potential, has a tradition going back through Heidegger to the pre-Socratic philosophers. Its importance for French structuralism is in showing that the junctures among structures have hidden places where power and desire can be hidden. The Greeks used the image of the fold to speak about self-love and how structures of the self are often doubled or folded back in order to provide security for the individual unsure about the political wisdom of working with others. Heidegger's Inquirer in *A Dialogue on Language* spoke about humanity holding "the two-fold of presence and present beings."[22] This "two-fold" is suggested by the Japanese word for "language": *koto-ba* (the delight of petals). The opening forth of blossoms is similar to the work of language as it relates the folds of an individual's presence in the world to the concomitant political reality of others sharing the same being and time and involved in Heidegger's structure of care. After Heidegger's revelation of the fold, it was the later Foucault who extended the notion of structure as "he created a new dimension, which we might call a diagonal dimension, a sort of distribution of points."[23] Once again, the word *fold* is crucial, both in Foucault's style, where the word recurs to reinforce its importance within his vision, and in his genealogical method whereby social families were created through the political expediencies of power groups folding in on themselves.

The "fold" can also be an image for a projection of social responsibility into the future. Deleuze would have us imagine a "superfold" that would have unlimited potential in time. He proposes that the double helix be the image for this superfold. In other words, if we study the operations of the double helix, we could better understand how to be in control of the being of language because the folds are perpetuated by language throughout history. The double helix, two intertwined strands around a cylinder observed as the structure of DNA, would become two straight lines if the cylinder were unfolded on a plane. This image has been useful for contemporary feminists to explain gender issues in a particular historical time warp when the female gender was folded under within larger male-oriented packages of values.[24] The double helix leads to Deleuze's theory of serial discourse as woven threads of meaning.

Deleuze and Serres Reinvigorate the Scientific Spirit

Gilles Deleuze and Michel Serres offered two different philosophical proposals for looking at the body politic in a mathematically inspired version of structure. Both were inspired by the philosophy of science and by Bachelard's insistence that the new calculations of mathematics contained the promise for the future ties between philosophy and science. The mathematical notion of a "series," an infinite number of things following one another and derived from a preceding element according to laws of succession, was adapted by Deleuze and Serres to each provide his own method for the philosophy of science to analyze a changing society.

Leibnitz, one of the forerunners of a French structuralism, also gave both of these intellectuals a point of departure for a mathematical model. Serres quoted Leibnitz's definition of a series as "technically, an arithmetic or algebraic sequence governed by 'reason' and, in the more universal meaning, any succession whatsoever of facts, events, reasons, or causes linked together by a law."[25] But it was Deleuze who first used the series to do what the static structure was incapable of doing: accounting for heterogeneity, the differences that fell by the wayside as structures linked similarities. Science, especially the topological studies of structuralist mathematics, offered the series as a way to explain time and different spaces. As opposed to Jürgen Habermas of the Frankfurt School for whom science had failed socially by not providing a model for human and social interests, Deleuze forged ahead to show that there was indeed a possibility to engage science in the task of social and political formation. And thanks to his insights, Foucault proposed that "perhaps one day, this century will be known as Deleuzian."[26]

It is too early to tell whether Foucault's statement is correct. Like the Enlightenment models, Deleuze's philosophy was not metaphysics but rather a close dialogue with the methods of science and mathematics. His studies of Kant and Leibnitz prepared us for his *Différence et répétition* in 1968 and *Logique du sens* (The logic of meaning) in 1969. The former distinguishes the major themes of philosophy as an alternation between the principles of repetition and difference. The latter introduces the series as a viable method for the philosophy of science. The series can be understood as a type of structure with the advantages of being able to account for the process of time while also explaining differences in systems of social organization. The serial form has the additional advantage that it has no shape, so that it is not bound to equilibrium, closure, or other geometrical conditions. It also has the infinite capability of being joined with other series through the use of "indeterminate objects."[27] This feature of the series, which Deleuze called the *objet* = x (the indeterminate factor),[28] is a common element in different series whereby a given series can link up with another series. This linking potential makes the series an attractive methodological tool for analyzing historical texts, social formations, and other items capable of being affected by historical change. The "indeterminate factor" can be used after the series is formed and provides an infinite number of possibilities for future adaptations.

Deleuze adapted the series as a model for philosophy's dialogue with science. He and Guattari proposed "schizoanalysis" as a way to account for disequilibrium in society. The neat charts of structures do allow us to investigate the systems in our lives. There is much to be said, however, about the chaos around and despite the systems. Schizoanalysis entails using the series to explain the nonsystematic presence of disorder in human lives. Humans are presented as "desiring machines," whereby both desire and machine are the operant concepts. Humanity is portrayed in *L'Anti-Oedipe* (*Anti-Oedipus*) as the experience of desire implementing an infinite "system of breaks" (the definition of "machine")[29] with the world.

Deleuze and Guattari thus portray human beings as having substituted technology for the Freudian triangulation of desire. Instead of the triangular structure of desire described by Lacan as the figurative or symbolic model for human thinking, the series describes the actual activity of desire by tracing its synthetic path through an alternation of connective, disjunctive, and conjunctive acts between individuals and their society. Schizophrenia has become the modern condition, as Deleuze told us that schizoid discourse is the one we all share: "All the words narrate a love story; but this story is no longer designated nor signified by words. It is caught up in the words, unable to be designated or signified."[30] The individual desires a social existence and encounters thereby the problems inherent to communication: the self being distinct from an Other.

Michel Serres promoted communication as an intersection of serial forms. Effectively, the "desiring machines" create disjunctions in the patterns of their lives as they attempt to connect with others. At those intersections of communication, individuals realize, with Serres, that "order is not the norm, but the exception."[31] In his study of Leibnitz (*Le Système de Leibniz*, 1982), Serres noted that classical thought had tried to create an order within infinity. It makes much more sense to allow for infinity and adapt to it.

Like Deleuze, Serres was opposed to psychoanalysis. His structural alternative was called "logoanalysis" and focused on intersubjective relationships whereby the individual was part of communicative networks. His proposal for the "invigorated scientific spirit" was an adaptation of Bachelard's vocabulary (in French, *le nouveau nouvel esprit scientifique* refers to the title of Bachelard's 1934 pamphlet *Le nouvel esprit scientifique*) and yet extended the mathematical set into a social form. Rather than fixed points of reference in human communication, "intersections" (in French, *interférences*) were interwoven references to the three networks of knowledge, the world, and the intersubjective human condition. In order to analyze these references, Serres posited three axes for the "invigorated scientific spirit": (1) informational thought (using thermodynamics as a model); (2) structural thought; and (3) the reflexive and critical dimension.[32] These three axes intersect over a single point in order to expand it, as in the image of a star or an asterisk.

By adding the third axis, Serres pointed to the necessity for French structuralism to become more reflexive about the human condition being described. History cannot be ignored as irrelevant. The very act of interpretation entails a historical dimension that the serial form can easily accommodate. The series offers the possibility for answering the question Serres asked of himself in sketching the program for logoanalysis: "Who am I? Certainly, nothing except the interceptor of theoretical knowledge, of the embryonic murmur of objects, of intersubjectivity which thinks according to the three intersecting networks."[33] Answering the question involves the admission that the structure is part of a political reality. To assess that reality, Serres proposed aligning the networks at a given intersection to identify the complex knot that we call communication.

As Serres and Deleuze continue to explore the existence of humanity at the intersection or on the fringes of the structures, they are also extending structuralism into the domain of semiotics to confront humanity "in charge of the being of language . . . the advent of a new form that is neither God nor man."[34] The test of the importance of the "reinvigorated scientific spirit" is in its ability to lead people intellectually into a new political era with the assistance of science and philosophy.

Chapter Eight
Toward a Universal Grammar

One of the claims of French structuralism was that truth is relational rather than abstract. This relational truth is similar to the relational structures found in language. Because of the cultural impact of French structuralism, grammarians, philosophers, and literary critics made concomitant investigations into the similar patterns between language and truth. This was especially the case in the area of narratives, as encouraged by the exemplary work of Roland Barthes, both in his proposal for a science of literature and in his later self-reflective memoirs. Narratives were a ripe area of study because of their inherent capacity to hold the interest of their listeners. This capacity entailed some sort of relational cohesion, sometimes called the syntagmatic axis by those influenced by the poetics of Roman Jakobson.

Jakobson had theorized that a literary text exists at the intersection of syntagmatic and paradigmatic axes. Basically, the syntagmatic axis is the combination of elements in any utterance, its narrative syntax. On the other hand, the paradigmatic axis is the deep level of an utterance, the semantic or discursive logic subtending what appears to be said in the narrative syntax. The intersection of these two axes represents the communicative act whereby six factors influence the message, which could be studied through the composition of a poetics relating the factors involved in communication.[1] But Jakobson's formalist background precluded studying the context for the linguistic message, except as one of the six factors.

Tzvetan Todorov expanded the Prague School's vision into the arena of narratology, whereby relationships rather than only elements of a narrative were studied. A Bulgarian by birth, Todorov published in French in Paris and provided crucial inspiration to others with his theory that there exists a "universal grammar" governing all languages and signifying systems and coinciding with the structure of the universe.[2] By its very nature of coincidence with the "structure of the universe," this "universal grammar" also dictates the structuring or twisting and turning (i.e., the tropes) of narrative discourse. Consequently, Todorov proposed a "narratology" to study the rules whereby storytelling is subject to a "universal grammar." His speculation was crucial not only in France (cf. Barthes, Gérard Genette, and Philippe Hamon) but throughout the world (cf. Gerald Prince, Seymour Chatman, Mieke Bal, and Lubomir Doležel). Todorov's Slavic background gave him access to the Prague School and to Russian formalism, whose works he presented to the French with his *Théorie de la littérature* (1965) and *Mikhail Bakhtine* (1981). It is important to note here that, although Lévi-Strauss distinguished structure from the form of the Russian formalists by stipulating that "structure" included both form and content, it was the Russian concept of form that inspired Todorov's narratological vision.

Todorov's prospectus for a "universal grammar" involved three subdivisions: the syntactic, the semantic, and the verbal. I will discuss studies by French structuralists in each of the proposed subdivisions. I will then look at the developments in analyses of storytelling by French structuralists, especially in the areas of narratology and the contextualist school of classical mythology. The syntactic research performed by Jean Dubois and his colleagues at Liège known as Group μ and by André Martinet is important for its taxonomic study of grammar, the discipline that looks at the structure of the sentence. In the area of semantics, A. J. Greimas was clearly the most influential writer, uniting research from the Prague, Copenhagen, and Yale structural linguistic schools to provide a transition for structuralism in the area of meaning into the field of semiotics. Thirdly, I will discuss the research in the art of verbal persuasion, rhetoric, as a consequence of French structuralism. In 1958, Chaim Perelman and Lucie Olbrechts-Tyteca announced a "new rhetoric" to replace those of Aristotle and Cicero. It was an ambitious undertaking reinforced by a sensitivity for stylistics in the work of Gérard Genette, who sketched the parameters for "the modern neorhetoric" with his series of books entitled *Figures*. This "rhetoric" became the basis for a good deal of narratological research.

The three subdivisions—syntax, semantics, and rhetoric—will provide the basis for examining which Russian formalists were important for narratology and why narratology itself was distinctive from the perspective of the three subdivisions. I shall present the works of the major French intellectuals in narratology, namely, Bremond, Todorov, Genette, and Hamon.

Finally, the French structuralists have also made major inroads in the study of classical mythology.[3] In the fifth and final section of this chapter, I shall examine the contributions of Jean-Pierre Vernant, Marcel Detienne, Pierre Vidal-Naquet, and Nicole Loraux to a distinctive "contextualist" methodology. These writers reacted to the Lévi-Strauss claim for the title "structuralist" by developing their own methodology for classical mythology. Led by Vernant who began at the École Normale Supérieure and moved on to the Collège de France, the others are mainstays at the École

Normale in the disciplines of history, classics, and ethnology, in which they have applied the study of myth.

Jean Dubois and Syntagmatic Structures

Jean Dubois and André Martinet were linguists who influenced the early development of French structuralism. Both provided theoretical models, Dubois in grammar and Martinet in phonetics. Dubois worked with several colleagues (Jean-Marie Klinkenberg, Francis Edeline, and Philippe Minguet) at the Université de Liège, publishing grammars under the pseudonym of Group μ and grammatical analyses under his own name. Martinet usually worked alone and from the early 1950s spread the word about advances in structural linguistics as well as about several of his own theories linking phonetics with meaning.

Dubois published the three-volume *La Grammaire structurale du français* in the mid-1960s, as a taxonomic effort to demonstrate the "profound dissymetry"[4] between the two codes of written and spoken French. This was to be a testimony to Jakobson's paradigmatic axis, because Dubois's examples of the supersegments of gesture and tone in the spoken language and the grammatical versus lexical marks of gender verified multiple levels of meaning. Dubois achieved notoriety, however, when Noam Chomsky[5] rejected the purported links between semantics and syntax offered by such probability models of grammar as those published by Group μ. Nevertheless, Dubois did provide insight into the redundancy of language with its duplication of marks for gender and number in the written language. He therefore proposed, as a way to minimize the noise thus produced between a sender and a receiver, a metalanguage to be developed lexically and provided in dictionaries for the users of specific languages.[6] Here, too, however, Dubois met with opposition, this time from Nicolas Ruwet, the French translator of Jakobson and a Belgian structural linguist. Ruwet identified Dubois with the Bloomfield or Yale School of structural linguistics because Dubois's taxonomies of language were too static and not predictive enough. He charged Dubois with the responsibility of being more sensitive to the rhetorical realities of popular spoken idiom than to the careful French language the Groupe de Liège had chosen to present.[7]

Martinet's phonetic research replied that communication was ensured despite the presence of noise in a given utterance. He observed that every phoneme has a field of possibilities to be realized, depending on the occurrence of the phoneme within differing contexts. Martinet's observations reinforced the mathematical theories of neighborhood by observing that sounds are always conditioned by their neighbors in a given communication system. For example, sounds may be voiced or agglutinated when two words come together in order to communicate verbally gender or number. Despite the apparent inertia of redundancy or noise in language, a certain economic transaction governs communication and ensures a mental energy whereby phonetic differences take place to make distinctions of meaning occur where they are needed. This theory by Martinet implies a certain innate order in language whereby relational structures occur for the organic integrity of the syntax of a language system. Martinet thus reinforced Jakobson's postulate of the syntagmatic axis as the primary determinant of meaning. Martinet's principle of "double articulation," whereby both meaning and vocal form are components of the same message, further corroborated syntagmatic structures as the predominant relationships in language systems.

A. J. Greimas and a Place for Semantics

Born in Lithuania, Algirdas Julien Greimas played a key role in relating structural linguistics to semiotics. His speciality is semantics, or as he would prefer to understand it, giving sense to meaning. His most influential works include *Sémantique structurale* (*Structural Semantics*) in 1966, *Du Sens* (*On Meaning*) in 1970 and volume 2 in 1983, *Maupassant* in 1976, *Sémiotique et sciences sociales* in 1976, and with J. Courtés, *Dictionnaire raisonné de la théorie du langage* (*Semiotics and Language*) in 1979.[8]

Greimas's purpose was to create an argument for semiotics as a science concerned with identifying "isotopes" in language. These isotopes are coherent units of logic gleaned from texts. For example, in *Sémiotique et sciences sociales,* he surveyed the social sciences to discover the "rational isotope" that functions as a metalogic to guide scientific discourse in its many manifestations toward the taxonomic inventory of truth. This isotope is formed as a type of social communication codifying its message, with a speaker (*destinateur*), and an audience (*destinataire*). Greimas believed that the assemblage of isotopes into a metatext could help us to understand the workings of human discourse. This metatext would then be useful as a map for how culture organizes meaning.

Greimas used both syntagmatic and paradigmatic axes to arrive at his various isotopes. In his *Maupassant,* for example, Greimas analyzed the short story "Deux Amis" (1883) in terms of these two axes as he sought the isotope for narrative discourse in the alternations of disjunctions and conjunctions. Through his discursive presentation of the integrity of these alternations, he claimed to have discovered a "profound textual isotope."[9]

His bipolar view of language thus reinforced Martinet's double articulation as well as the dualisms innate to language as described by Saussure, Hjelmslev, and Benveniste. Greimas went further, however, by diagramming the various poles with mathematical precision and then discussing the unity of the syntagmatic and paradigmatic chains of meaning within the isotope. In a well-documented presentation of Greimas, Ronald Schleifer pointed out that the semantics of Greimas combines the strengths of the Prague, Copenhagen, and Yale schools to achieve a unity of method with the isotope.[10] The methodological unity presents diagrams of correspondences among themes that serve as spatiotemporal coordinates for the continuity of the intrigue within a story. The narrative act of telling a story thus becomes analagous to the cognitive and pragmatic act of deciphering the meaning of a story.[11] By setting up this analogy, Greimas provided a model for structuralism in time, what Fredric Jameson called a "genuine hermeneutics."[12] This model is "genuine" in that Greimas did not postulate some spatial idea of structure but rather dealt with the reader's problem of identifying meaning during reading.

Greimas called his model "actantial analysis" because he distinguished, in narrative analysis, the syntactic players (*actants*) from the actors to whom words are attributed. The syntactic players in a narrative are mapped in order to demonstrate the differences between what a subject means and what the words say. Greimas transcended the binary opposition so characteristic of structural linguistics to present the logical powers of these players to combine and to contrast. Borrowing the logical paradigm of the square of opposition as a model for his "semiotic square," he mapped meaning in such a fashion to show that signification entailed complementary, contrary, and contradictory relationships to the contextual setting of a text and its culture. Through the rigor of his logical approach to meaning, Greimas pointed to the possibility that isotopes, bundled together, could provide a metatext that would give us hints about the unity of the algorithm of language. He did not, however, complete that task[13]; the logic in that task was passed on to narratologists. Meanwhile, rhetoric was clamoring to replace logic with what Schleifer identified as "the characterizing difference between 'structuralism' and 'poststructuralism.'"[14] Rhetoric is also another name for the third subdivision in Todorov's prospectus for a universal grammar. Now that we have seen the conjectures of French structuralism about syntax and semantics, let us look at the revival of rhetoric and the ensuing formation of a poetics of narrative.

Rhetoric and the Acts of Speech

The political failures of French structuralism provided a social direction for the study of language. Rhetoric offered an attractive way of linking words with their audience since historically it was the science of persuasion, as taught by Aristotle or Cicero. Barthes, however, observed that the verb "to write" had become an intransitive verb.[15] The conscious intent of the speaker was no longer appropriately conveyed by the language of the writer. Todorov noted that the study of this type of classical rhetoric (*inventio, dispositio,* and *elocutio*) was no longer an effective means of studying language.[16] Quintillian and Demosthenes, however, had provided an alternative for rhetoric as the science of eloquence, whereby tropes and figures of speech were studied in themselves as part of the *scientia bene dicendi* (the science of speaking well).[17] This latter view of rhetoric focused on the act of performance, which Émile Benveniste would present in 1958 as the key to understanding the functioning of language.[18]

The year 1958 saw also the publication of *La Nouvelle Rhétorique* by Chaim Perelman and Lucie Olbrechts-Tyteca. Their title announced an age wherein rhetoric would become increasingly important for the study of French language and literature. Meanwhile, at Oxford University, J. L. Austin discovered speech-act theory, which examined interpersonal communication through identifying the rules for the classification of speech acts, that is, what is accomplished in the act of speaking. Speech-act theory became influential because of its reproduction of interpersonal relationships in language. Barbara Herrnstein Smith expressed this focus of speech acts appropriately: "We perform verbal acts as well as other acts, that is, in order to extend our control over a world that is not naturally disposed to serve our interests."[19]

Meanwhile, in France, Oswald Ducrot brought the influence of speech-act theory into the company of Todorov, who collaborated with him in 1972 to produce the *Dictionnaire encyclopédique des sciences du langage,* an overview of the predominate interests of language study. Their collaboration was significant because the rhetoric of speech acts was similar to the poetics advanced by the Russian formalists, which Todorov had himself rejuvenated in France in 1967 with his *Théorie de la littérature*. Jakobson had isolated six features of a communicative act: its sender, receiver, message, code, context, and contact. These six features provide the parameters for an utterance and define its plural nature.

Maurice Blanchot and Jacques Derrida expanded on this plural nature of the speech act. Blanchot provided the philosophical and critical underpinnings of the plurality of language. He traced back to Wittgenstein the mathematical properties of this insight "recognizing that speech is necessarily plural, fragmentary, and capable of continuously maintaining difference beyond unification."[20] This "difference" is the innate power of language to defer recovery of its meaning. Blanchot's literary criticism focuses on texts whose language constantly postpones meaning by fooling the reader, whose gaze does not see the "true" meaning of the words. This is so because there is no single "true" meaning. The reader is actually blinded by the apparent vision of the text's message.[21]

With Derrida, there is a methodological break with French structuralism that begins with his rhetorical claims in *De La Grammatologie* (1967) that "language, passion, and society . . . constitute the movement of complementarity whereby these poles are substituted in turn for each other and whereby emphasis is begun in articulation and is fragmented by the distances it achieves."[22] Quite a mouthful, even for Derrida. His insights here are numerous. First of all, the triangulation of language, the individual ("passion"), and society creates the parameters for the situation of rhetoric as the predominant discipline in his method called "deconstruction." Derrida gives the speech act the crucial site where the emphasis can be placed on one of the poles he identified. Most important of all is the act of fragmentation that continuously keeps the "poles" of the triad spaced apart in time and place. The images of holes, fragments, gaps, and abysses are found throughout the works of Blanchot and Derrida to express the lack of relationship among speaker, words, and receivers in writing. Ultimately, this "lack" would lead to the replacement of French structuralism by perspectives that aspire to fill the void it was incapable of seeing because of its limited focus on the linguistic model.

Through the rhetorical studies of French structuralism, the field of poetics was revealed as a rich arena for further study. Poetics is the internal theory of the constitution of literature. Hayden White, an American historian, pointed out that, in the wake of Foucault, the human sciences themselves were revealed to have a poetics, that is, "a genuine 'making' or 'invention' of a domain of inquiry, in which not only specific modes of representation are sanctioned and others excluded, but also the very contents of perception are determined."[23] History, economics, psychology, and the other human sciences are telling stories being narrated by certain storytellers for certain listeners. Their stories are imbedded in language that has its own logics. *Logics* is plural because language can be literal or figurative and can consequently have entirely independent and even contradictory meanings. Paul de Man therefore noted the importance of our understanding that "rhetoric radically suspends logic and opens up vertiginous possibilities of referential aberration."[24]

Of course, these possibilities were always there. It is just that French structuralism permitted us to understand that the singular force of an incisive, all-pervasive logic within language was an illusion.

Gérard Genette had an especially perceptive vision for rhetoric. He advocated "the modern neo-rhetoric,"[25] which studied the figurative nature of language, not merely the metaphorical representation that grammarians such as the Groupe de Liège[26] advocated but the "focalization" (point of view) inherent to stories. Genette distinguished three imbedded speech acts in every narrative: the story (*l'histoire*), the narrative discourse (*le récit*), and the narrating situation (*la narration*).[27] These three distinctions have cleared the way for thinking through the ramifications of the poetics of narratives, narratology. The relationships among the three operative speech acts have generated considerable debate. Genette himself stipulated that time (order, duration, and frequency) and mood set the tone for the ties between the story and its narrative discourse, whereas voice governed the relationships between the narrative situation and the story as well as between the narrative situation and the narrative discourse. And yet he knew well that it was the act of narrating that was the key to the whole rhetorical situation: "The passage from one level to another can only be theoretically ascertained by the narration, the act which consists precisely in introducing into a situation, by means of a discourse, the knowledge of another situation."[28] That act of narration leads us into a whole world whereby discourse is focalized, despite intentions otherwise.

Tzvetan Todorov and the Development of Narratology

The Russian formalist Vladimir Propp had analyzed folktales in 1928 in his *Morphology of Folktales*. He used the term morphology to point out that the use of a form is a choice about an interpretive model of reality. Lévi-Strauss objected to Propp's presentation as being syntagmatic rather than paradigmatic, that is, being too concerned with the linear succession of events (syntax—hence, syntagmatic) rather than with the more profound "structure" underlying the choices of the forms. But not everyone agrees with Lévi-Strauss, who constantly overlooked the obvious in favor of complex hidden meanings. The rhetorical writers appeared to be opposed to the grammatical and syntactical analysts. The syntagmatic analysis of narratives was increasingly attractive to those who understood narrative as a grammatical exercise (e.g., Gerald Prince, in his *Grammar of Stories,* 1973).

Claude Bremond (b. 1929) also was a grammarian of narrative. Whereas Propp had defined thirty-one "functions" as acts of "a character, defined from the point of view of its significance for the course of the action,"[29] Bremond objected to this view as teleological, that is, its beginning was justified by the end of the story. Instead, Bremond appeared to be a throwback to Sartrean existentialist views of narrative, in that he proposed a series of choices in the plot as strings linking bifurcated moments. He focused on the choices of the characters as "the narrative goes into a series of imbedded episodes, each intermediate task being the means of another one."[30] The end of the narrative is precisely that for Bremond, the end of these strings of choices, the attainment of a stasis, the termination of tension for the characters. Propp would have the end be a determination as to how the various forms of the narrative "function" with each other. Bremond, however, argued that the moments of choice are the moments of structure or classification for the narrative. As Culler has noted,[31] Bremond departed here from the lessons of structuralist linguistics about the importance of context. Indeed, he was heading in a different direction, that of humanistic value given to choices and to acts rather than to endpoints and teleology. A narrator can indeed orient a story toward a particular didactic ending. But to present the narrator in this manner, according to Bremond, is to fictionalize the work of storytelling and to take the narrator out of real experience.[32]

But Bremond's insights were themselves limited by his intention to analyze the "narrated narrative."[33] He understood narrative to be finished in the sense that its story was already told. On the other hand, Genette and Greimas viewed narratives as still being narrated to the degree that listeners and readers are continually hearing and reading what the story says. In a seminal essay for the development of narratology, Roland Barthes revealed the tension of these two positions in the differentiation between the "translatable" and the "nontranslatable" elements of narratives.[34] Meanwhile, he was working on the "translatable" elements by parsing a short story by Balzac called "Sarrasine," and in 1970, published his results in a book called *S/Z*. He succeeded in showing how the story could be reduced to five codes woven together in such a way that they are still a testimony to his vision of how a literary form is constructed. The issue of *Communications,* published by the École Pratique des Hautes Études in 1966, in which Barthes's essay appeared, is now a classic because it also contains essays by Greimas, Bremond, Umberto Eco, Christian Metz on film, Todorov on categories of literary narratives, and Genette on the limits of narratives. Narratology would soon be pronounced by Todorov (*Poétique,* no. 3, 1970) as having an independent existence with enough major intellectuals defining its parameters to give it the presence of "critical mass" (in the physicists' sense of proximity to explosion). The French journal *Poétique* joined ranks with *Poetics* (the Netherlands), *Poetics Today* (Israel), and *New Literary History* (the United States—University of Virginia) as forums for debating the translatable components of narratives.

Todorov became very active in his project to compose a "universal grammar" of narratives. He seemed to be attracted to the "untranslatable" or immutable character of the narrative as he sought to delineate a poetics of narrative. For him, a poetics entailed laws or rules by which stories are narrated. He examined the formal properties of narratives in search of this poetics.[35] At one point (*Recherches poiétiques,* vols. I and II, 1976), Todorov adopted Paul Valéry's term *poietics* to describe the concern with the dynamics of the text's constant progress, its continual search for formal identity. During this exploration of *poietics* in the place of poetics (a term implying a static understanding of the text as a congealed unity), Todorov isolated a textual rule called "endogenesis" (as opposed to "exogenesis," the external determination of a story), whereby an internal dynamics gives the cohesion to a text such that the presence or absence of a single element is self-referential. Genres thus become important because each genre possesses different principles of endogenesis, and, as Todorov told us, different "horizons of expectations" for readers.[36]

Todorov brought with him to Paris a whole tradition of Soviet lore in the area of formalism. In addition to Propp, he rekindled the study of other Russian formalists such as Tynianov, Eichenbaum, Shklovski, and Tomachevski, who were theoreticians of narrative. These writers also reminded the French of the importance of the Prague School and Roman Jakobson, who had emigrated to the United States and become an important structuralist voice emanating from the Massachusetts Institute of Technology.

Meanwhile, Tynianov's writings reaffirmed the serial method, promulgated by Deleuze and Serres. Tomachevski focused on the sequence of clauses in a narrative, whereas Shklovski preferred order to sequence in identifying the succession of clauses in a story. In addition, Todorov was instrumental in placing Mikhail Bakhtin's thought within the French forum (*Mikhail Bakhtine: le principe dialogique,* 1981). Bakhtin (1895–1975) coined the terms *chronotope* (a time/space category), *heteroglossia* (the primacy of context over text), and *carnivalization* (the popular tradition of comedy in narratives) in a system of thought whose full implications for narratology are still being explored.[37] Thus, there was clearly a strong Slavic influence in the development of narratology. But Todorov also selected rhetoricians and specialists in hermeneutics (*Théories des symboles,* 1977) to arrive at a series of theoreticians of discourse who intuited the symbol as a key to understanding figurative language. He observed that "every society, every culture has a discursive ensemble which we can analyze and form into a typology (*la typologie*)."[38]

This "typology" would result from the systematic collection of rules for each "discursive ensemble" that is already being analyzed. Jurij Lotman, a contemporary Soviet semiotician from the State University of Tartu whose work is well known to the French, has theorized that a text transforms its culture into "a hierarchy of codes which have developed during the course of history."[39] The hierarchy is an abiding concern of his Tartu School semiotics defining the interaction of texts and cultures.

French structuralists, however, have also been focusing on the description, rather than the universalization, of what happens in narratives. Influenced by Greimas, Philippe Hamon (*Introduction à l'analyse du descriptif*, 1981) understood typology to be a semantic grid for helping us to see what happens in the descriptions contained in stories. For example, description becomes for him a narrative technique for imbedding ideology, which is "a relationship inscribed in the text and constructed by it."[40] Indeed, narratologists are convinced that the inner order of a story is paramount. Influenced by Genette's internal focalization of stories, Gerald Prince has developed insights into the "narratee" (*Narratology*, 1982), Mieke Bal has produced her own *Narratologie* (1977), and Susan Lanser, *The Narrative Act* (1981). Many more are to follow,[41] thus applying Todorov's view of *The Quest of the Holy Grail* to all narratives: "So that if the author could not quite understand what he was writing, the tale itself knew all along."[42]

The Vernant Group and the Contexts of Myths

As a specialist in classical mythology at the École Pratique des Hautes Études, Jean-Pierre Vernant was greatly influenced by the anthropological techniques of Lévi-Strauss to understand myth as part of a network of stories within a culture. Although the "homologies" of Lévi-Strauss were attractive because they created intersections not apparent within a myth taken as a separate story, the linguistic models were even more seductive for Vernant because he studied classical Greek myths united by the same language. Lacan's concentration on Poe's "Purloined Letter" revealed an insight by the character Dupin, who solved the problem of the purloined letter by conceiving of mathematics differently than the local police. This was an insight appropriate for mythologists as they pondered whether to adapt the structuralist method: "The great error lies in supposing that even the truths of what is called pure algebra are abstract or general truths. . . . There are numerous other mathematical truths which are only truths within the limits of relation."[43] A similar error is conveyed by Lévi-Strauss who, according to Vernant, provides a misleading structuralist model suggesting that "it is possible to decipher a myth even without a knowledge in depth of the civilization that produced it."[44]

What intrigued Vernant and his colleagues much more was the analysis of the Asdiwal myth, whereby Lévi-Strauss introduced the "ethnological context" as a methodological model for myth analysis.[45] Marcel Detienne, a philologist at the École Pratique, presented this latter model by Lévi-Strauss as worthy of being emulated in the study of classical Greek myths because of its thorough presentation of the contexts of the human sciences prior to the actual analysis of a myth. Vernant and Detienne organized a group of scholars at the École Pratique specializing in Greek mythology to foster the contextualist approach to "structuralist" analysis. This group was brought together as the Louis Gernet Center. It also included the historian Pierre-Vidal Naquet (b. 1930) and the sociologist Nicole Loraux (b. 1943).

These intellectuals were generally more sensitive to the geographical and historical contexts of Greek myths and mores. They adapted the linguistic models of Lévi-Strauss to the litmus test of history, thus demonstrating, as Loraux notes, that "the reading of a text is nourished by a constant interaction between its contents and its context."[46] Whereas Detienne tended to focus on the ensemble of Greek mythology (e.g., *Les Jardins d'Adonis,* 1972; *The Gardens of Adonis*) and to see individual myths as functioning within that context (e.g., *Dionysos mis à mort,* 1977; *Dionysos Slain*), Vernant understood the context as the intellectual heritage of the Greek culture. For example, he and Detienne collaborated (*Les Ruses de l'intelligence,* 1974; *Cunning Intelligence in Greek Culture and Society*) in a presentation of the value given in Greek mythology to *mètis,* cunning intelligence. Vernant's larger vision may have been responsible for his ultimate election to the Collège de France, whereas the other members of his contextualist group remain on the faculty at the École Pratique.

The *contextualist* term was devised by Vernant as meaning that any message implied a necessary involvement between an interlocutor and an audience. The precise application of the context was then determined by a given myth understood as a "speech act" at the intersection of historical and geographical factors that are isolated as appropriate. The message of the myth was a crucial focus for the contextualist group. Its definition was attained through the study of the interaction of the story with its culture. Detienne noted the distinctive type of structuralism practiced by the contextualist group, in saying that "the mythologist's structuralist models cannot do without the analyses of the historian: without them their coherence and logic would have no foundation."[47]

Pierre Vidal-Naquet has been an especially articulate historian within the contextualist group. Particularly effective in bringing political attention to the atrocities committed in the Algerian War (*La Torture dans la République,* 1962; *Torture: The Cancer of Democracy*) and then to the anti-Semitism surrounding the Arab-Israeli Six-Day War (*Les Juifs,* 1981; *The Jews*), he is a historian inspired by the "structuralist" mode to study the practices of slavery, the rule of women, and adolescent rituals within ancient Greek culture. He discovers the similarities and interrelationships among these classes of people (*Le Chasseur noir,* 1981; *The Black Hunter*) as pariahs in their societies, inasmuch as they were subject to castigation within the myths and rites of those societies. Vidal-Naquet's chief contexts are the political and ideological substrata left unsaid in the classical Greek stories narrated as part of the daily rituals of the city dwellers.

Nicole Loraux focuses on the Greek attitude toward death as the context for the myths that were spun about life. She portrays the Greek funeral orations as opportunities for ideologies to be spun about the city-state by confusing life and death among the listeners who were mesmerized by the rhetorical deliveries. Loraux reveals the gaps between what was said about the Greek way of life at these moments and what actually happened during daily interactions. She is especially concerned with the myths about children and women. Like Detienne and Vernant (*La Cuisine du sacrifice en pays grec,* 1979; the sacrificial cuisine in Greece) and Vidal-Naquet, Loraux does poignant research into the Greek portrayal of the condition of women. She discovers that the lack of heroic deaths for women was part of a larger Greek attitude relegating women to silence and thus exclusion from the storytelling dimension. Her insights reflect Jean-François Lyotard's awareness of a skepticism about metanarratives in his *La Condition postmoderne* (1979) so that "most people have lost the nostalgia for the lost narrative."[48] Some of the French structuralists, however, believed that they could retrieve that nostalgia by using structuralist principles to identify first-order narratives.

Chapter Nine
First-Order Narratives

Structural linguistics made claims for itself as the scientific analysis of language. The Cartesian scientific tradition had previously given the French a model for thinking based on the priority Descartes gave to thinking ("I think, therefore I am"). French structuralism tried to unite structural linguistics with Cartesian science. But the blend was not a smooth one. Foucault, for example, noted that "the reason it is now so necessary to think through fiction—while in the past it was a matter of thinking the truth—is that 'I speak' runs counter to 'I think.'"[1] The awareness that thinking had to be filtered through language thus created a suspicion about what language was doing to thought. Jurij Lotman of the Soviet Tartu School called language a "secondary modeling system" because of what the structuralists had revealed to him. As a result of this space between language and truth, there were some writers among the French structuralists who preferred to examine alternatives to language in order to delineate the primary structures of human behavior.

These writers who narrated those first-order samples of French structuralism were considered exponents of "genetic structuralism." Jean Piaget, Lucien Goldmann (1913–1970), and René Girard (b. 1923) come to mind for their constructions of first-order models as French structuralism was on the wane. Their interventions were called psychological, Marxist, and mythical, respectively. Piaget was Swiss. Goldmann was born in Rumania and came to Paris in 1934 after his education in Vienna. Girard was born in Avignon, but his academic career has been with universities in the United States.

Jean Piaget was a biologist by training who made great strides in developmental child psychology in Geneva with his method called "genetic structuralism." His interdisciplinary tendencies were exceptional in the field of psychology, as he preferred to work with teams of specialists from other sciences because he claimed to need these people to contradict him from outside his area of competence.[2] From children's behavior, Piaget theorized about cognitive "structures" that imitated mathematical models and authenticated interactions between psychological and biological functioning. For him, "structures" were "organic coordinations"[3] between an individual's activities and a perceived object's reactions. Since Saussure had assigned the determination of the exact place of semiology to the psychologist,[4] Piaget took it upon himself to set the record straight that mathematics identified the patterns and structures for all of nature. Cognitive and biological structures are then analogical reproductions of mathematical structures. This observation was the basis for Piaget's elaboration of what had become known as structuralism. His *Structuralism* is a very clear and coherent exposé of the methodological principles advocated by many structuralists.[5] Its publication in 1968, coupled with the political crises in May of that year, give it a curious place in the history of French structuralism. Although the document does not discuss many French structuralists outside the realms of mathematics and the natural sciences, the cohesion of the document made structuralism a definable intellectual and methodological force against which many young avant-garde writers would react in their sympathy with the frustrated challenges of the May 1968 revolts. Although Piaget intended to rally the cause of structuralism around common traits with a mathematical base, he ironically sounded the death knell by alerting intellectuals to a name with which they should henceforth not be associated. We have already noticed the reluctance of Foucault, Deleuze, Serres, Lotman, and others to be identified with the label although their methods and presuppositions were clearly structuralist.

Also adopting the "genetic structuralist" designation was Lucien Goldmann, a sociologist at the École Pratique des Hautes Études. Since Goldmann was primarily a Marxist, some critics (Todorov, Fredric Jameson) do not include him as a structuralist. He was intent, however, on demonstrating how humanity generates structures along class lines. He identified himself as "a sociologist, a man of science who tries both to do concrete research and to isolate a positive method for the study of human and social facts."[6] This method was inspired by Marx, Piaget, and Georg Lukács (1885–1971). For Goldmann, the primary model for structure was the class to which an individual belongs and which provided a worldview whereby the individual interacts ideologically and epistemologically with the environment. In opposition to the positions of Lévi-Strauss and Barthes about the structuralist project, Goldmann preferred the evolutionary applications of Piaget's "genetic structuralism."

René Girard, trained as a historian, also was called a "genetic structuralist" by Goldmann; the latter may have preferred a coalition of scholars to oppose the likes of Barthes and Lévi-Strauss. Nevertheless, Girard was very distinctive in his concerns as he asserted: "I reject the frame of current theory, and I deliberately reintegrate the banal and traditional framework of scientific research."[7] His type of science is the scholarly pursuit of a mythic mentality concerned with the modeling of mimetic desire. He studied Greek society where violence was justified in religion through the practice of sacrifice. Therein he observed the pattern of the links between desire and violence that has been repeated throughout Western culture.

Jean Piaget: The Claim for the Sciences

Jean Piaget was first to make the claim for "genetic structuralism." The word *genetic* contradicts the universal nature of structure as Lévi-Strauss and Barthes conceived it and as the early Foucault presented it in his archetypal studies (e.g., *Les Mots et les choses*). Piaget was inspired by the evolutionary nature of biology to reconcile history with the mathematical structures found in the experimental sciences. These sciences were Cartesian, for Piaget. Their roots were in mathematics and in the assumption of a constructed subject. In Piaget's *Biologie et connaissance* (Biology and learning) in 1967, he postulated the existence of "isomorphisms," that is, analogies, between organic and cognitive processes. He was no philosopher and reproached philosophy for claims to attain knowledge without verification. Instead, he preferred knowledge based on "collective verification by means of controls mutually agreed upon."[8] With this method, he studied how an individual passes from a lesser to a greater degree of knowledge relative to the level and perspective of the subject. He theorized stages through which children evolve as they mature into adults. These stages thus account for a sequential "genesis" of the structures of knowledge (genetic epistemology).

Although Piaget insisted that his method accounted for the interaction between the subject and its environment, Lacan spoke of the "Piagetic error,"[9] whereby the egocentric discourse of the child was the basis for the reciprocity between cognitive structures and the environment. Piaget's method was thus understood as underscoring that developmental psychology had the key to structuralism, because it studied change while assuming the integrity of the thinking, knowing subject. Of course, psychoanalysts such as Lacan also had an axe to grind with their criticism of psychology. Between the two camps of psychology and psychoanalysis lies the strength of Piaget's contribution. His research is important for placing the "structure" of the French structuralists into historical context. His "structure" was much more adaptable and subject to change over time. With this in mind, let us review the parameters he laid out for structuralism in 1968.

Piaget's prescription of structuralism was incisive and inflated all at once. He identified a critical choice for the identity of a structure as either a static form or a system of transformations. Of course, Lévi-Strauss would have said that structure was a combination of form and content. But Piaget concentrated on the distinction of static versus changeable. He gave examples from mathematics, physics, biology, and psychology to characterize three major traits of a structure: its wholeness, its capability for transformation, and its self-regulation. A structure's wholeness is identified by the relationships among its constituents and marks its distinctiveness from a mere collection of contiguous elements. This universal aspect of structure is shared by all structuralists as the distinction of structure from themes, atoms of meaning, form, or other bases for looking at the consistency or integrity of life.

The second feature, being able to change, identifies Piaget's vision for a genetic structuralism. The structure must be able to engender other stages in a pattern of growth. Of course, Piaget received much opposition as he tried to make analogies from his biological view of organic structures to epistemic and intellectual structures. His theory was that the Bourbaki mathematics was a key to unlocking the transformational character of logic that was supported by Chomsky's School of Generative or Transformational Grammar. Since the Bourbaki had elaborated on the Erlanger Program, a proposal to change geometry into the study of elastic shapes,[10] their mathematics was one of maximum generality in order to allow for the generation of any mathematical concept from a set of common properties. This mathematics thus gave Piaget the basis for linking the biological and the psychological into one theory of genetic structuralism. He even thought that a gestalt "is mathematizable insofar as it is reducible to probability diagrams."[11] Hence, patterns of behavior could be traced to mathematical models as the sources for all structures.

Thirdly, self-regulation maintains the integrity and closure needed for a structure to operate as an identifiable unit. Structures have innate laws governing the relationships of their components and the "nesting" of form and content. This "nesting" is achieved through the principle of equilibrium, whereby a balance is achieved between form and content for the survival of the structure. And yet this self-regulation must also have something similar to Freud's death instinct, because the structure does change and become something else. Piaget's model for knowledge as a spiral enables us to visualize the coherence of each spire changing over time in contrast with the structure of a building: "Rather than envisaging human knowledge as a pyramid or building of some sort, we should think of it as a spiral the radius of whose turns increases as the spiral rises."[12] Of course, objections continue to be made about why the spiral must "rise." Does this mean that knowledge always leads to progress or to some teleological end? Even within developmental psychology, there is still considerable debate about whether Piaget's genetic structures are as universally valid and self-regulated as he would have them be.[13]

Piaget's genetic structuralism tended to ignore the role of factors external to structures in modifying the structures. As opposed to the nonconscious structuring of humanity and its world elaborated by Lévi-Strauss, Piaget gave humanity a much more active and optimistic role in the creation of structures: "Man can transform himself by transforming the world and can structure himself by constructing structures; and these structures are his own, for they are eternally predestined either from within or from without."[14] The "predestination" of the genetic structures from without is not obvious in Piaget's presentation of the stages of cognitive development; he did engage specialists of other disciplines to work on that part of his theory. Lucien Goldmann, a sociologist, adapted Piaget's genetic structuralism with theories from Marx and Lukács to develop an explanation of the outer predestination of evolving structures. The narrative of the evolving subjective self lacked an elaboration of its social setting, and Goldmann met this need.

Lucien Goldmann and Class as a Significant Structure

The primary principle of structures for Lucien Goldmann was social class. He borrowed Piaget's term "significant structure" and applied it to social class acting as a totality or whole within which an individual generated structures. As opposed to the Cartesian scientific method of learning from the simple to the complex, Goldmann advocated an interactive epistemology, adapted from Piaget's principle of assimilation and accommodation, whereby "the progress of knowledge proceeds . . . from the abstract to the concrete through a continual oscillation between the whole and its parts."[15] The individual was thus presented with a "transindividual" consciousness whereby a Piagetian-type equilibrium between a thinking subject and a social class is attained. Similar to the Bakhtinian vision promoted later by Todorov and Kristeva, Goldmann defined this "transindividual" as "the subject made up of several individuals."[16] The transindividual consciousness transfers the values of the group into a vision of the world for all to discuss. It was Goldmann who, in 1966 at a conference on structuralism at Johns Hopkins University, noted that "aesthetic value belongs to the social order; it is related to transindividual logic."[17] The Many thus find their voice in the transindividual One who speaks through their mask on their behalf.

Goldmann tempered Piaget's version of genetic structuralism with adaptations of Marx and Georg Lukács. Lukács was a twentieth-century Hungarian intellectual, whose work was celebrated for its radical Marxian critique of bourgeois culture. His "world vision" would mark Goldmann's entire presentation of genetic structuralism. After Goldmann studied law at the University of Bucharest, he went to Vienna where he encountered the writings of Lukács, predominantly in German. Goldmann was particularly struck by Lukács's *History and Class Consciousness,* from which Goldmann decided that Marxian analysis of society, culture, and economy was all-important. Goldmann specifically gleaned from Lukács an appreciation for structure intimately linked with history. The key was a concept Lukács called "totality," explained thus: "The all-pervasive supremacy of the whole over the parts is the essence of the method which Marx took over from Hegel and brilliantly transformed into the foundation of a wholly new science."[18] Lukács had thus transferred to Goldmann crucial concepts to be debated and adapted by the various ideologists of French structuralism. The supremacy of the whole over its parts was what Lévi-Strauss would call "totalizing," and it would generate considerable methodological debate from Jean-Paul Sartre in the early 1960s because of its Kantian overdetermination of a structure. Lukács also gave importance to Marx's "new science," promulgated by Louis Althusser's Marxian structuralism. And Roland Barthes would object in his *Sur Racine* to "confusing" history and structure in this "genetic" type of structuralism.

Genetic structuralism became a literary method in the sociologically oriented writings of Lucien Goldmann. In *Le Dieu caché* (*The Hidden God*), he promoted a method that focused on social class as the primary generating influence on the literary structures of Pascal and Racine. This was an early example of a structural, sociological method. He narrated the stories of transindividual subjects (Pascal and Racine) who had visions of the world representing the collective consciousness of the seventeenth-century French groups the Jansenists and the *nobles de robe* (holders of high judicial or legal office upon whom aristocracy was conferred). The values of these French religious and social classes profoundly affected how Racine and Pascal presented the interactions of humanity and God. These literary examples demonstrate, according to Goldmann, that humanity generates structures along class lines and that genetic structures are necessarily functional.

Thus, Goldmann set himself apart from French structuralism once again by stipulating, along with Piaget, that structures had functional meanings. Jean Hyppolite, the noted French historian, took Goldmann to task for the lack of universal evidence that structures had to be functional.[19] But Goldmann was not one to be deterred by a simple objection. He had given other examples of the functional meaning of genetic structures by analyzing the works of Malraux, Genet, and Robbe-Grillet in *Pour une sociologie du roman* (Toward a sociology of the novel) in 1964. Goldmann also stated that this functionalism underscored three principles in relating the individual to a social class: (1) it demonstrated the human tendency to adapt to a milieu; (2) it exemplified the human tendency toward coherence and the formation of global structuring processes; and (3) it showed the dynamic character of human behavior in being able to modify the nature of a structure.[20]

Like Piaget, Goldmann maintained that genetic structuralism was able to account for change through a dialectical relationship between history and structure. He observed that "the problem of structure is also a problem of levels."[21] To deal with this, he adapted Piaget's notion of isomorphisms, analogies between the biological and the psychological orders, to what he called "homologies," whereby levels of meaning explained such dialectical pairs as subject/object, theory/praxis, and structure/history. These homologies are structural parallels whereby stories can be told on different levels and linked up by analogy. By creating these horizontal levels, however, Goldmann precluded the functional relationships of the "vertical" subtexts within each of the stories told on separate levels. The effect was to deny formalists (Fredric Jameson[22]) or semanticists (A. J. Greimas) the functional analyses of subtexts.

But Goldmann focused on texts whose meanings were not dependent on the functioning of the subtext. Even more annoying than Goldmann's choice of great, coherent texts to analyze was his method. For example, Serge Doubrovsky observed that "Goldmann's method proceeds from ambiguity to clarity too easily."[23] This procession was based on Goldmann's theory that genetic structuralism had the dual purpose of being explicative and comprehensive. On the one hand, his method had to explain the relationships between the significant structure and its constituent elements or subordinate structures. This was a purpose addressed to the inner workings of the great, coherent texts of literature. On the other hand, the comprehensive vision of genetic structuralism had to include the various levels within which the text functioned. In this way, the factors external to literature would account for the phenomenon of "structuration" that Goldmann described as stemming from "the fact that individuals and their social groups attempt to make unitary and coherent responses to the problems posed by their milieu."[24]

The "unity" and "coherence" of these responses were too easy, however. Goldmann had a vision for a first-order narrative combining history and structure, but it was not complex enough to explain social interaction. His method was called "monistic" in its presentation of social structure[25] and too symmetrical and mechanistic a model[26] for wide application outside the tragic visions of selected seventeenth-century (Pascal, Racine) and twentieth-century (Genet, Robbe-Grillet, Malraux) writers.

Another "genetic structuralist" offered the expansive vision lacking in Goldmann. Ironically, Goldmann himself described René Girard as a genetic structuralist while not being aware that Girard would survive him and broaden the scope of the term Goldmann had introduced into the study of literature.

Girard and the Mythical Triangulation of Mimetic Desire

In a 1959 conference at Cerisy-la-Salle, France, Jacques Derrida raised an objection to Goldmann's method by explaining that he could not understand how a scientist of empirical reality (a sociologist) could also provide a science of the subjective vision of a writer. Goldmann answered: "It can happen that the observer of the outside may at the same time be the one who sees the structure from the inside."[27] The problem of inside/outside was thus resolved by stating that one can be both. But that seemed too naive an answer for Derrida, who developed the theory that the inside meaning is the only one there is.

Meanwhile, the literary critic René Girard was using his training as a historian to explore the beginnings of storytelling in the Bible and in Greek tragedy. There he observed the triangulation of the subject/object relationship with the introduction of a mediator, thus giving intersubjective reality complex spatial dimensions. Girard told a story within this space about what he called "mimetic desire," as opposed to the linear procession of simple subject-object desire. This phenomenon is the subject of his first-order narrative, which encompasses not only Greek myths and biblical stories but also fiction by such novelists as Stendhal, Proust, and Dostoyevsky, among many others.

Basically, mimetic desire is desire patterned on what another person wants. The closer one gets to obtaining the object of desire, the more one begins to hate the imitated other. The double bind between the imitator and the imitated generates violence throughout history. This violence is sanctioned in religion through sacrificial rites and in society through the scapegoat, which Girard calls "the generative principle of mythology."[28] Of course, it is the critic's role to be the mediator as a storyteller, "to expose to the light of reason the role played by violence in human society."[29]

The desire to be like the other determines social behavior, in Girard's opinion. He has traced the existence of this mimetic desire as a mythic mentality common to most of Western civilization. By ascertaining mimetic desire as the triangular "family of models"[30] for violence, sacrifice, and scapegoating, he provided a generative pattern for explaining structures and history within a paradigm of conflict. Girard himself noted that "the classical structuralists repress conflictual mimesis as much as anyone did,"[31] because of their insistence on static models of structure.

His proposal dealt with conflict as the heart of social struggle and the violence that ensued from this struggle. He built a series of models generated from the double bind at the core of the triangular structure of imitative desire. The imitator and the imitated are in a dynamic tension because of the common object of their desire. This tension characterizes some of the great novels in history, such as *Madame Bovary* by Flaubert, *Le Rouge et le noir* (*The Red and the Black*) by Stendhal, and *Crime and Punishment* by Dostoyevsky. As Girard saw the protagonists of these great novels, their self and their other were two apparently different thrusts of their desires. Their victories, if they occurred, were in the realization of the unity of self and other in that desire. The strength of these analyses lies in their capacity to present the unity and the diversity of human endeavors without being either oversimplified, as was Goldmann's signifying structure, or so historically determined that the analysis was only valid for a limited number of samples, as with the Jansenist tragic world vision examined in Goldmann's presentations of Pascal and Racine. Instead, Girard's vision is panoramic because, as Burton Mack understands Girard, "he wants, after all, to account for the entire sweep of human history in relation both to its origins and to its eventualities."[32]

In this generous "sweep," Girard linked biblical tales, Greek myths, and great novels by building mimetic desire into the driving force for sacrificial rituals and especially scapegoating. He noted that sacrifice was the most crucial and common type of ritual that reproduces violence within a religious and controlled setting. Ironically, although his models were generative in that they accounted for many cultural narratives, his ultimate purpose was to establish "a typology of the stereotypes of persecution."[33] Curiously enough, the typology was the method used by Barthes (*S/Z*) and Todorov (*Introduction à la littérature fantastique*) and criticized for its inability to deal with changing or evolving historical and social struggles.

Girard inverted the process by using change as the method with typology as the end result. The changing effect of mimetic desire on the various types

of narratives throughout history results in Girard's conclusion that scapegoating is the generative principle of mythology. He would have us believe
that "the scapegoat process is so powerful that it turns its victim, in the eyes of
the persecutors, who are also mythmakers, into a transcendental symbol not
only of violence and disorder, but of peace and order as well."[34] This
surrogate-victim mechanism that he identified is well documented, with examples from throughout history.

Nevertheless, the examples do not constitute a linear influence or tradition; this mimetic desire is a structure, after all. Girard himself noted that, by
the very fragmented and discontinuous nature of structures, his study of victimization had to be theoretical: "The structuring power of victimization is
necessarily hypothetical because no continuous line of empirical evidence, no
linguistic-structural analysis will ever lead to it."[35]

And so what we have is a first-order narrative by Girard that is structural
without a language model and genetic without the need for the controlling
subject of Cartesian science. Girard's portrayal of the victim as a transcendent
symbol of the enduring structure of mimetic desire laid the groundwork for
the dialogue between French structuralists and the German hermeneutic philosophers. The result would be the natural evolution of French structuralism
into something other than itself.

Chapter Ten
Mapping the Path Taken

The many players discussed in this book blazed the path of French structuralism from the 1950s until the 1980s, when we can surely say that it has run its course and is being superseded by other attitudes about life. As we have seen, the word *structure* was etymologically derived from the Latin *struere,* signifying the noun "building" or the verb "to build." The concept of structure was adapted from the fields of grammar and biology, where the classifications of syntax and the systemic life networks of biology influenced the adaptations of structuralism in other disciplines. Whereas the noun *building* refers to such types of structuralism as the taxonomic schemes of Bloomfield's immediate constituent analysis focusing on a structure that is already there or "built," the verb *to build* characterizes the French schema of constructing the various relationships of parts to wholes. For example, in 1963, Roland Barthes called structuralism the activity of humanity fabricating its own meanings.[1]

This French structuralism, however, did not by any means provide a single way of understanding the verbal sense of "fabricating meaning." Borrowing a heritage beginning with Descartes and looking back variously to Spinoza, Leibnitz, and such pre-Socratic philosophers as Democritus, Heraclitus, and the Pythagoreans, the French structuralists had many differences separating them. Why call them by the same name (structuralist) at all? In their defense, they did have some common bases, besides historical ones. They were all working with the premises of the Hegelian dialectic, that is, the teleologically directed and totalizing combination of opposites (thesis/antithesis/synthesis). Self and other were dialectically related, as with Lacan's presentation of the thinking subject. Sometimes the direct influence was Marx; most often it was more subtle but Hegelian in its teleological plan nevertheless.

The work of the French structuralists was also commonly characterized by a search for a hidden order beneath the surface; for example, in Althusser's *Trager,* the class members are the supports for class struggle. In addition, Paris and the French language provided a common identity as "French" structuralists. Ironically, as mentioned earlier, many of the French structuralists were not of French origin (Lévi-Strauss, Greimas, Todorov,

Althusser, Goldmann, etc.). Therefore, the relationships of inside/outside and parts/whole were natural ones to explore. The "dynamic tolerance" proposed by Lévi-Strauss is an example of the promotion of such relationships on a pluricultural scale. These relationships set up the structures that were related to larger networks or systems. Meaning, rather than cultural artifacts or objects, was an abiding concern to explain connections, so that the discourse was often abstract, for example, Greimas and his explanation of semes and isotopes. And the plural fragment was a stylistic device (e.g., the later Barthes, essays by Lévi-Strauss) focusing attention on the antihumanistic tone of much of French structuralism. Antihumanistic meant that there was a shift from the monocultural implications of one, indivisible humanity toward the relationships of groups affecting each other for better (e.g., the myths suggesting a "human spirit" according to Lévi-Strauss) or for worse (e.g., the hegemonic ties between power and knowledge revealed by Foucault).

And yet French structuralism leaves us with a sense of plural efforts made in heterogeneous directions. Let us recapitulate where the individuals who made these efforts have taken us, in order to appreciate their originality, their shortcomings, and their heritage for the present and coming generations. Unlike surrealism, which had André Breton to shape and direct its philosophy and ideological concerns, French structuralism did not have one, single voice uniting its evolution. Instead, there were five proponents, whom I have called its "ideologists" and who provided leadership in five separate disciplines and blazed a trail for others to follow. This trail was marked by two common traits: the ideologists' desire to provide a map for French structuralism and their concerns with the scientific model. After discussing the identity of the ideologists, the mapping strategies that ensued, and the role of science in the aftermath of French structuralism, I will conclude with observations on how the limitations of French structuralism are being explored by the revival of semiotics as a humanistic discipline.

The Ideologists despite Themselves

Ideology is not the conscious construct that philosophy is. Instead, ideology is a set of values, often expressed unconsciously as a network of ideas that predispose others to think in a certain way. Within French structuralism, ideology had its way, even though the major writers objected to their identification as ideologists and would have agreed with Lévi-Strauss that they were "masked" by their common grouping as structuralists.[2] Nonetheless, they often gave interviews as structuralist ideologues whose complementary responses led to a single historical phenomenon. Yet there was no single canonical method that came out of this grouping. And despite themselves, each of the five major writers was responsible for an ideology about the nature of change, that is, an explanation of how structures became manifest to them after being hidden for so long from others.

We have seen the ethnologist Lévi-Strauss present *bricolage* as a way to resist monocultural hegemony. Rather than the engineer's use of science to construct a framework from a blueprint, bricolage was a collection from various cultures of myths, masks, kinship systems, incest taboos, and other artifacts in order to discover a model of the human spirit. His ideology was one of "dynamic tolerance," whereby the method of the "ethnological context" retained the cultural integrity of a people while also explaining how cultures transform their stories from those of other historical moments and geographical places. The nonrecursive myths and the nontranslatable components (*indécidables*) provided testimony to the tolerance needed to allow each culture its own voice. And the structures that a culture had in common with another culture was then part of a larger system of communication. Lévi-Strauss promoted the plotting of such systems on horizontal and vertical axes, thus encouraging the maps and geometries of communication systems.

Althusser, however, understood the systems identified by Lévi-Strauss as types of theoretical hegemony in themselves. Hence, he promoted a theory of social transformation gleaned from a symptomatic reading of Marx. Such a reading focused on Marx's proposal for a new science, not to develop the philosophical implications for economics or to realize an ideal such as the human spirit, but rather to portray class struggle and the spatial structures of social configuration. For Althusser, the simple structure of class struggle was to be found in the complex ways societies organized themselves. The crucial method in this discovery was Marx's new science of history, which would retain the focus on the struggles rather than on the systems of human communication.

And yet for Foucault, the systems of thought remained important, as he promoted an ideology that portrayed historical struggles for power in knowledge. His progression from archaeology to genealogy and to topology traced the problems of change from a question of masks in archaeology, with its probing of the depths to reveal a treasure hidden by layers of matter, to a genealogy whereby groupings by family trees reveal the genetic coding that time has hidden, and finally to a topology whereby the arrangement of masses of information reveals the order and sequence in which transformations take place. For Foucault, structures were revealed through the discovery of palimpsests in history. By exposing those areas of human struggle erased historically, Foucault portrayed a society much more hegemonic than it had considered itself to be.

This authoritative presence was explained psychoanalytically by Lacan, whose ideology manipulated time by explanations of the father's presence in the symbolic. By arranging the dialectical meeting of self and other into a triangular model, Lacan effectively displaced the thinking subject by subverting its conscious control and integrity. Like language, the self is in constant flux, never able to fix its location, always reflecting the authority of the law, the symbolic, the father. But the flux of the subject imitated the future perfect tense of verbs (e.g., "I will have become"). And Derrida, although a critic of Lacan, also spoke of the future perfect tense as appropriate for the voice of the displaced subject. As Heidegger proposed the future perfect in *Being and Time*, that tense unites past and future so that change is a prospect whereby being can examine itself without the sequence of past-present-future to hinder thinking by forcing it into a linear, successive mode.

Barthes characterized the whole structuralist experience by proposing the ideology of reading obliquely. At first, the "science of literature" promised that poetics or narratology could lead him to understand how the structures of texts presented themselves. His writings after *S/Z* (1970), however, revealed a sensitivity to his physical involvement in what he had proposed as the study of how we mentally experience structure through reading.[3] The involvement of desire, its frustration, the angles of the manifest meaning relative to the writer and to the reader, and the "middle voice" of the writing itself became crucial components in his presentation of the life of language, differentiated from either the writer or the reader. The appearances of a fragmented form in his later works pointed to an essential ingredient of structural literary analysis as he once described it: "The stake of structural analysis is not the truth of the text but its plural."[4] Indeed, the surface contained more of the structure than many had assumed; the trees were being forsaken for the forest by the abstract ideologists of French structuralism. It was up to the mapmakers of French structuralism to depict the trees ignored by the ideologists with their teleological visions.

The Geometries of Space

Once the ideologists of French structuralism had presented their visions of what structures could offer, other French writers began to examine how self-reflexive these visions were. Each of the ideologists had many major disciples. We have seen some of these, for example, Clément and Leach (disciples of Lévi-Strauss), Todorov and Kristeva (Barthes), Jacqueline

Rose and Jacques-Alain Miller (Lacan), Deleuze and White (Foucault), and Cambrier and Fraschira (Althusser). But the mirror stage so widely promulgated by Lacan was not so universal in its appeal. One problem with the mirror stage is that it assumed a whole self capable of looking into the mirror or seeing others as distinct.[5] Hence, some French structuralists saw the tain worn off the back of the mirror, so that no reflection of their own condition was possible in the mirrors of the ideologists. Instead, the problem was noting where there were reflections and where one could see through the looking glasses of these ideologies and present maps for navigating the confusing new terrains of French structuralism.

It was Althusser who noted that the materialism of the modern age had to provide a space for society. The ideologists provided the ideological overlays for this space, what Richard Harland called "superstructures." Structural linguistics had provided the parameters of binary principles with synchrony/diachrony, signifier/signified, *langue/parole,* and other distinctions to set up polar boundaries. Jakobson, Hjelmslev, and Lévi-Strauss then used horizontal and vertical axes to plot these binary principles. Lévi-Strauss, followed by Foucault and Deleuze, added a diagonal or third axis to this chart as a tertium quid not able to be enclosed by polar distinctions.

The widely used grid relied heavily on two-dimensional charting. But the geometry of structure had to be more complex for some of the French structuralists. Alternatively, Lacan used the image of the rebus or picture puzzle to map the decentered ego being triangulated. That same triangle reappeared with Girard's explanation of mimetic desire. And Greimas went one step further with the semiotic square to explain the logical possibilities of meaning. It was Foucault's topology that revealed these types of structures as closed. Their closed nature shut out representatives of humanity despite society's claim to be humane and humanistic in its structure. Space had become restrictive because of its shape. Foucault recalled Heidegger's concern with the fold of memory as a crucial image in mapping our future investigations. Once again, the future perfect is a time in which the memory of the past would enable us to make the future open to change and to Lévi-Strauss's "dynamic tolerance" of difference.

The Model of Scientific Reason

French structuralism began with a claim to scientific reason. Linguistics had just assumed its identity as a social science. Lévi-Strauss saw himself as a man of science, the ethnologist who used empirical examples and mathematical models. Lacan was a medical doctor. Barthes called for a "science of literature," a poetics to analyze the rhetorics of writing and reading. Foucault's archaeology was a determined effort to place epistemology on the level of a science. And Althusser claimed Marx's "new science" as the harbinger of a political science without equal.

But the role of science in French structuralism was more ambiguous than it first appeared. It was Roland Barthes who first observed, in 1964, that the work of Lévi-Strauss questioned the language and the manner of scientific reason itself.[6] Since primarily philosophers responded to a query by Barthes and the *Annales* staff to evaluate the impact of Lévi-Strauss on the human sciences, the result was a debate about the philosophical parameters of scientific reason. This debate especially focused on *La Pensée sauvage,* in which Lévi-Strauss defended his totalizing method in the face of charges by Sartre that the ethnologist was not dialectical in his approach. Indeed, Lévi-Strauss was not dialectical, but admittedly Kantian. Of course, Barthes would also turn his back on the science of literature and prefer an alternative to the Hegelian-inspired notion of science so popular in France immediately after World War II. The dialectic of Hegel seemed to so enrapture French intellectuals that science was not possible without engaging in some sort of tension between self and other, as Sartre had accused Lévi-Strauss of not being an authentic scientist because of the absence of dialectical thinking. French structuralism would be caught up in this questioning of the Hegelian dialectic and also the implied lack of concern about others or society in its "scientific" identification. The binary distinctions of structural linguistics fed into the Hegelian method. But as the limitations of the language model became more and more obvious, the dialectic would become antidialectical by revealing the limitations of teleologically oriented, polarized models of human thinking.

Lacan continued the questioning of scientific reason as he publicly doubted that psychoanalysis was a science. His use of hypnosis to control his analysands during sessions increased suspicions about his selection of a shaman's tricks rather than the tools of medical science. In addition, Lacan continually asserted that the thinking subject was not verifiable. Hence, empiricism was of no use in his practice. The structures he identified, although based on Freud's own dialectical distinctions such as those between conscious/unconscious, displacement/condensation, analyst/analysand, and self/other, went beyond the Hegelian model by being generated from his triangularized confrontation of the real, the imaginary, and the symbolic in the thinking subject. Also, in his reflections on the problems his model posed for feminism, he began to reconnect the body and the mind, so long separated in distinct realms since Descartes. For example, Lacan was celebrated for saying that woman does not exist. The woman he spoke of is the intellectual category from the point of view of the symbolic order. Since the unconscious is structured like a language and the syntax of language is constructed by men, there is no unique way for language to express woman except as a dialectical opposite of man, which is simply a negation of itself. One positive insight derived from this statement was that Lacan was postulating the interconnections of body and mind so that language would have to be restructured as a parallel endeavor to the new freedoms of women's bodies. In that way, women would have their own language in the manner that Hélène Cixous, Irigaray, and the feminists of Psych et Po have advocated in the recent past in France.

Foucault, on the other hand, understood a cleavage between his words and his thought. His body was not necessarily united to his words. But, just as the later Barthes observed that his words had a physical existence separate from his desires and his body, so could Foucault reiterate, as we have already seen, that "'I speak' runs counter to 'I think.'" Foucault's observation became more desperate when he admitted that "I am fully aware that I have never written anything other than fictions."[7] The scientific knowledge that lies could be produced despite the intention to say the truth was a crucial discovery resulting from French structuralism. Effectively, science was portrayed as subservient to narrative.

Structures, however, were not capable of accounting for disequilibrium or hierarchies at different sites. Hence, the Hegelian dialectic had still regulated the conceptualizing of structure even though science itself was shown to be deficient. Descartes and Hegel were strong presences for the writers of French structuralism. The shadows of these two philosophers were so encompassing that knowledge and social welfare were separated technocratically for the pursuit of intellectual ideals. The poststructuralists had to seek other philosophical traditions (the Stoics, Heidegger, Adorno) in order to retrieve social welfare and incorporate it into the agenda for a scientifically inspired analysis of communication within a cultural setting. Here, semiotics could meet the need.

The Semiotic Web

As French structuralism eventually created its own demise in its reliance on the modeling of language systems and on the bankrupt Hegelian dialectic, semiotics was beginning to be recognized worldwide as an enterprise that could rise out of the ashes of structuralism. The term *semiotics* was invented by the Stoic philosophers and given a disciplinary identity by the American pragmatist Charles Sanders Peirce (1839–1914) and most recently by Thomas Sebeok and Umberto Eco, among others. In France, Louis Marin, Christian Metz, Georges Mounin, and Julia Kristeva have been the primary exponents of semiotics as a freestanding field of study.

There has been some confusion between "semiology" and "semiotics," as to which name should be used. Saussure had noted that linguistics was part of the larger system of signs called "semiology." In 1965 (*Éléments de sémiologie*), Barthes inverted the relationship by stipulating that semiology was part of linguistics and should be studied as a language system. Hence, *semiology* became the appropriate word for such a sign system subservient to the language model. And *semiotics* became the study of communication systems, with language as only one of those operative systems.

Once the teleological projection of the dialectic was revealed as bankrupt because of the hegemonic threats of totalizing unities, the French poststructuralists were left looking for models to study communication. Certain affirmations remained, despite the rejection of the Hegelian and Cartesian oversimplifications. Whereas Jean Baudrillard offered an apocalyptic vision with the Beaubourg Museum in Paris functioning for him as "the monument to the simulation games of the masses . . . as an incinerator absorbing all cultural energy and devouring it,"[8] there were also positive projections of a renewed innocence of "libidinal economy" (*Économie libidinale,* 1974) by Jean-François Lyotard in esthetics. Greimas echoed Lyotard's affirmation by pointing out that "the so-called esthetic values are the only clear-cut ones, the only ones that while refusing to be negative pull us upward."[9] Semiotics, however, does offer another possibility between these two extremes of apocalypse and impossible innocence, the former a modern nihilism and the latter a totalizing reprise of the past.

This third possibility, semiotics, is not a form of Hegelian synthesis. Instead, Theodor Adorno (1903–1969) of the first-generation Frankfurt School proposed the "negative dialectic" as an anti-Hegelian manner of understanding history and communication. Peter Dews has affirmed the importance of Adorno for poststructuralism: "In opposition to interpretations of reality as a temporal movement towards ever more complex and differentiated forms of integration and reconciliation, Adorno argues that the historical process must be understood as advancing both towards less and less mediated forms of unity, and towards increasing antagonism and incoherence, because of the abstraction built into the instrumental use of concepts, which idealist philosophy overlooks."[10] In effect, within semiotics, the "negative dialectic" can be used to study the effects of the subverted linguistic model of communication.

The semiotics of Julia Kristeva is especially noteworthy. Her *chora,* as a prediscursive materiality, points toward the poetic potential of communication. Such poetry would use open-ended strategies to implement a vigilant subversion of the symbolic's authoritative presence in communication, especially for women but also for men sensitive to the hegemony of the father and the law.

The "dynamic tolerance" advocated by Lévi-Strauss would be especially useful in guiding the recognition of Derrida's *différence* as the effect of the negative dialectic examining the many abstractions about language and semiology made in the idealist spirit of French structuralism. There is a certain pragmatism in this promotion of a dynamic tolerance. Curiously enough, that pragmatism can be observed in Jacques Derrida's work and certainly in the American philosophical traditions from Peirce through William James to the contemporary Stanley Cavell. Peirce insisted that, instead of dyadic relations emphasized by linguistic and epistemological models, communication should be viewed as a triadic relation whereby human choice rather than determinism is highlighted. As John Sheriff stated recently, "Peirce emphasizes that humans are freed, rather than enslaved by language."[11] This focus on human freedom could also help draw humanists back into intellectual discussions after being ejected by the antihumanistic claims of Lévi-Strauss, Foucault, and Althusser. Through the application of the values of French structuralism, there is much potential for the French to join the long-ignored pragmatic traditions of the United States.

Ironically, French structuralism has bequeathed a series of values linking intellectuals to civic consciousness. Despite a certain hermetic aloofness commonly associated with this group of writers, the failure to involve the general population in its concerns has generated a reaction, a call for ethical discussions about social responsibility. Michel de Certeau, Bernard Henri-Lévy, and Jean Baudrillard have written as if they were standing on the shoulders of Foucault (voices for marginalized groups), Althusser (struggles as the focus of social change), and Goldmann (class as a significant structure) to involve intellectuals in linking knowledge to social welfare. The French are involved in worldwide discussions (e.g., Jean-François Lyotard, Richard Rorty, and Jürgen Habermas on postmodernism) about the stakes in these issues, so that the cultural identification of French with French structuralism may nevermore be an issue. The cultural and social issues now at stake are part of international and humane settings, rather than restricted to a language, a city (even one as cosmopolitan as Paris), or a nation. Semiotics has become a concern for modern fiction writers,[12] as Lyotard proposes that "dissensus" (*Le Différend,* 1983) be preferred to Habermas's consensus between intellectuals and society because the intellectual has a leadership role to play in making people think.

At the very least, there is an awareness of political life and the ties that bind cultures and societies. That semiotic web has strands that change shape and may now be spun in an ever-widening arc. The French structuralists were responsible for analyzing an area of that web known as language. It is now up to others to expand on the subject matter of the French structuralists and to integrate their reflections into our understanding of human communication.

Notes and References

Chapter One

1. Lévi-Strauss himself rejects the alliance of these names in a common venture called structuralism. He would rather have his name associated with a tradition beginning with Georges Dumézil and Émile Benveniste and continuing with Jean Pierre Vernant and his colleagues of the Centre de Recherches Comparées sur les Sociétés Anciennes at the École Pratique des Hautes Études (now called the Gernet Center). See the Lévi-Strauss interviews with Didier Eribon in *De Près et de loin* (Paris: Odile Jacob, 1988), 105 ff.

2. Foucault gave many interviews about his dissociation from the word *structuralist*. Especially after the May 1968 student-worker rebellion in France, "structuralism" became identified with the pre-May 1968 political and academic attitudes. Foucault's star began to rise as he associated himself with the new academic regimes and proposed a poststructuralist agenda therein. As an example, see his interview in "Structuralism and Post-Structuralism," *Telos* 16, no. 55 (Spring 1983): 195–211.

3. Frank Lentricchia, *After the New Criticism* (Chicago: Chicago University Press, 1980), 109 ff.

4. Jonathan Culler, *Structuralist Poetics* (Ithaca, N.Y.: Cornell University Press, 1975), 7.

5. Roland A. Champagne, "Anti-Structuralist Structures: The Avant-Garde Struggles of French Fiction," *Studies in Twentieth Century Literature,* no. 1 (Spring 1977): 135.

6. Jean Pouillon noted that "structuralism" was effectively "in style" when he attempted to define what it was in a special edition of *Les Temps Modernes* in November 1966.

7. Edward Said, "Abcedarium Culturae: Structuralism, Absence, Writing," in *Modern French Critics,* ed. John K. Simon (Chicago: Chicago University Press, 1972), 378: "Recent French critics focus on fixed 'structure' rather than the processes of 'structuring.'" The study by Roland Barthes in *S/Z* (Paris: Seuil, 1970) exemplifies the first position, heavily influenced by the American Bloomfieldians and promoted by the *Tel Quel* journal. The second position was especially elaborated by the *Change* Collectif, founded by Jean Pierre Faye in 1968 and elaborated in the Paris-based journal *Change*. On the one hand, the system reigns (Saussure). On the other hand, the process of language determines the system (Hjelmslev).

8. Jean-Marie Benoist, *The Structuralist Revolution* (London: St. Martin's Press, 1978), 2 ff.

9. Émile Benveniste, *Problems in General Linguistics,* trans. Mary Elizabeth Meek (Coral Gables, Fla.: University of Miami Press, 1971), 8.

10. Mikhail Bakhtin's work in the Soviet Union is now being discovered and appreciated for its reaction to the structuralist movement. In his *The Dialogic Imagination,* ed. and trans. Michael Holquist and Caryl Emerson (Austin: University of Texas Press, 1981), 426, he defines chronotope as "an optic for reading texts as X-rays of the forces at work in the culture from which the text springs."

11. Justin Lieber, *Structuralism: Skepticism and Mind in the Physical Sciences* (New York: Twayne, 1978), 8.

12. Claude Flament, "L'Étude mathématique des structures psycho-sociales," *Année Psychologique* 58 (1958): 417.

13. See, for example, the Group μ's *A General Rhetoric,* trans. Paul B. Burrell and Edgar M. Slotkin (Baltimore: Johns Hopkins University Press, 1981), as the Group seeks to outline the basic principles composing all figures of speech. The Group μ was directed by Jean Dubois and included F. Edeline, J.-M. Klinkenberg, P. Minguet, F. Pire, and H. Trinon. Their work is discussed in chapter 8.

14. Benveniste, *Problems,* 21.

15. Jean-Marie Benoist, "Structuralism: A New Frontier," *Cambridge Review* 93, no. 2204 (22 October 1971): 17.

16. Claude Lévi-Strauss, Paris colloquium, 10 January 1959, in *Sens et usages du terme structure dans les sciences humaines et sociales,* ed. Roger Bastide (The Hague: Mouton, 1962), 143.

17. Elmar Holenstein, *Roman Jakobson's Approach to Language: Phenomenological Structuralism,* trans. Catherine and Tarcisius Schelbert (Bloomington: Indiana University Press, 1976), 13 ff.

18. Franz Brentano, *The True and the Evident,* trans. R. Chisholm et al. (London: Routledge & Kegan Paul, 1966), 71.

19. Roland Barthes, *Essais critiques* (Paris: Seuil, 1964), 213.

20. Rudolf Engler, ed., *Saussure's "Cours"* (Wiesbaden: Otto Harassowitz, 1967).

21. See Jonathan Culler, *Ferdinand de Saussure* (New York: Penguin, Modern Master Series, 1976), for a discussion of the plural Saussures. The Columbia University–based journal *Semiotext(e)* would have two Saussures, one dealing with the priority of linguistics, the other of semiology, as the dominant models for communication (see vol. 1, no. 2, Fall 1974, ed. David Neiger and Sylvère Lotringer).

22. For example, Brentano remarked that the word *color* has the grammatical form of a noun but does not refer to anything existing in the real world. See his *The True and the Evident,* 71.

23. Jean Piaget, *Structuralism,* trans. Chaninah Maschler (New York: Harper Torchbooks, 1979), 76.

24. Ferdinand de Saussure, *Course in General Linguistics,* ed. Wade Baskin (New York: McGraw-Hill, 1966), 13.

25. See representative translations of his work in *A Baudouin de Courtenay*

Anthology: The Beginnings of Structural Linguistics, ed. Edward Stankiewicz (Bloomington: Indiana University Press, 1972).

26. Fredric Jameson, *The Prison-House of Language* (Princeton: Princeton University Press, 1972), 18.

27. N. S. Troubetzkoy, *Principles de la phonologie,* trans. J. Cantineau (Paris: Klincksieck, 1949), 11.

28. Saussure, *Course,* 112.

29. See the discussion by J. G. Merquior, in his *From Prague to Paris: A Critique of Structuralist and Post-Structuralist Thought* (London: Verso, 1986), and the review by Roland A. Champagne of his work in *World Literature Today,* Spring 1987, 355.

30. See "Les Thèses de 1929," *Change,* no. 3 (1969): 23 ff., for a presentation of the basic tenets of the Prague Circle.

31. Bohumil Trnka et al., "Prague Structural Linguistics," in *Structuralism: A Reader,* ed. Michael Lane (London: Jonathan Cape, 1970), 73.

32. Holenstein, *Roman Jakobson's Approach,* 13.

33. Roman Jakobson, "Action," in his *Selected Writings,* vol. 2 (The Hague: Mouton, 1971), 711.

34. André Martinet, "Function, Structure, and Sound Change," *Word* 8 (1958): 1–32.

35. Roman Jakobson, "Linguistics and Poetics," in *Style in Language,* ed. T. Sebeok (Cambridge: MIT Press, 1960), 358.

36. See the English translation in *The Structuralists from Marx to Lévi-Strauss,* ed. Richard and Fernande DeGeorge (New York: Anchor, 1972), 124–46.

37. Michael Riffaterre, "Describing Poetic Structures," in *Structuralism,* ed. Jacques Ehrmann (Garden City: Doubleday, 1970), 188–230.

38. Jakobson, "Action," 711.

39. See Todorov's *Recherches poïétiques,* 1 and 2 (Paris: Klincksiek, 1976); Roland A. Champagne's review of it in *World Literature Today,* Winter 1978, 188; and Todorov's *Introduction to Poetics,* trans. Richard Howard (Minneapolis: University of Minnesota Press, 1981).

40. See Roland A. Champagne, "A Grammar of the Languages of Culture: Literary Theory and Yuri Lotman's Semiotics," *New Literary History* 9 (Winter 1978): 205–220, for a discussion of the stakes in Lotman's theories.

41. See Roland A. Champagne, "The Problem of the One and the Many: A Case for the *Change* Collectif," *Boundary 2* 4 (Spring 1976): 917–23, for a detailed account of the creation of the journal *Change.*

42. Louis Hjelmslev, *Prolegomena to a Theory of Language,* trans. Francis J. Whitfield (Madison: University of Wisconsin Press, 1969), 55.

43. See Ronald Schleifer's discussion of the intellectual context for Greimas in *A. J. Greimas and the Nature of Meaning: Linguistics, Semiotics, and Discourse Theory* (Lincoln: University of Nebraska Press, 1987).

44. Noam Chomsky, Review of B. F. Skinner's *Verbal Behavior,* in *Language* 35 (1959): 26–58.

45. See John Lyons, *Noam Chomsky* (New York: Viking, 1970), for a discussion of Chomsky as a "physicalist" within the context of the Cartesian body-mind problem.

46. See Roman Jakobson, "Linguistics and Communication Theory," *Proceedings of Symposia in Applied Mathematics* 21 (1961): 245–52.

47. Nicolas Bourbaki, *Algèbre commutative* (Paris: Hermann, 1961), 41.

48. Mikhail Bakhtin and P. Medvedev, *The Formal Method in Literary Scholarship* (Cambridge: Harvard University Press, 1985), 134.

49. Louis Althusser, *For Marx,* trans. Ben Brewster (New York: Pantheon, 1969), 229.

50. Claude Lévi-Strauss, *The Savage Mind* (Chicago: University of Chicago Press, 1966), 247.

51. Michel Foucault, *The Order of Things* (New York: Vintage, 1973), 385.

52. Jean Pouillon, "Un Essai de Définition," *Les Temps Modernes* 22, no. 246 (November 1966): 774.

53. A. M. Métailié, ed., *Les Années Soixante en noir et blanc* (Paris: Éditions A. M. Métailié, 1980), 153.

Chapter Two

1. See Roland A. Champagne, *Claude Lévi-Strauss* (Boston: Twayne World Author Series, 1987), for a more elaborate discussion of Lévi-Strauss haunted by his otherness.

2. Claude Lévi-Strauss, "L'Analyse Structurale en Linguistique et en Anthropologie," *Word* 1 (1945): 33–53.

3. Claude Lévi-Strauss, "Ce Que Je Suis," *Le Nouvel Observateur* (28 June 1980): 15.

4. Lévi-Strauss, "L'Analyse Structurale," 48.

5. Simone de Beauvior, Review of *Les Structures élémentaires de la parenté* by Lévi-Strauss, *Les Temps Modernes* 5, no. 50 (November 1947): 947 ff. Jane Gallop acknowledges the debt of feminism to this insight by Lévi-Strauss into the male domination of women's sexuality through kinship systems in her *Daughter's Seduction* (Ithaca: Cornell University Press, 1982), 133.

6. Jean Piaget, *Structuralism,* trans. Chaninah Maschler (New York: Harper Torchbooks, 1979), 110.

7. Claude Lévi-Strauss, "Les Mathématiques de l'Homme," *Esprit* 24, no. 10 (1956): 525.

8. Edmund Leach, *Claude Lévi-Strauss* (New York: The Viking Press, 1970), 103.

9. Lévi-Strauss, "L'Analyse Structurale," 50.

10. Claude Lévi-Strauss, *Leçon inaugurale* (Nogent-le-Rotrou: Daupeley-Gouverneur, 1970), 44–45.

11. Claude Lévi-Strauss, "Réponses à Quelques Questions," *Esprit* 322 (November 1963): 640.

12. Claude Lévi-Strauss, "Lévi-Strauss en 33 Mots," *Magazine Littéraire,* no. 223 (October 1985): 27.

13. Claude Lévi-Strauss, his contribution to a colloquium in Paris in January 1959, in *Sens et usages du terme structure dans les sciences humaines et sociales,* ed. Roger Bastide (The Hague, Mouton, 1962), 150.

14. Sanford S. Ames, "Structuralism, Language, and Literature," *Journal of Aesthetics and Art Criticism* 32, no. 1 (1973): 90.

15. Jacques Derrida, "Nature, Culture, Écriture," *Cahiers pour l'Analyse* 4 (September-October 1966): 10.

16. Claude Lévi-Strauss, "L'Anthropologie Sociale devant l'Histoire," *Annales: Économies, Sociétés, Civilisations* 15, no. 4 (July 1960): 628.

17. Mary Douglas, "The Meaning of Myth," in *The Structural Study of Myth and Totemism,* ed. Edmund Leach (London: Tavistock, 1967), 67.

18. Claude Lévi-Strauss, "Le Temps du Mythe," *Annales: Économies, Sociétés, Civilisations,* no. 26, 3 (1971): 533 ff.

19. Raymond Bellour, "Entretien avec Claude Lévi-Strauss," in *Claude Lévi-Strauss,* ed. Raymond Bellour and Catherine Clément (Paris: Gallimard, 1979), 166.

20. Claude Lévi-Strauss, *Anthropologie structurale* (Paris: Plon, 1958), 364.

21. Jean-Paul Sartre, "Jean-Paul Sartre Répond," *L'Arc,* 6, no. 30 (1966): 90.

22. Lévi-Strauss, "Les Limites de la Notion de Structure en Ethnologie," in *Sens et usages,* 45.

23. André Green, "La Psychanalyse devant l'Opposition de l'Histoire et de la Structure," *Critique* 19, no. 194 (July 1963): 661.

24. Lévi-Strauss, "Ce que Je Suis," 17.

25. A good analysis of the stakes for Lévi-Strauss and Sartre is given by Lawrence Rosen in "Language, History, and the Logic of Inquiry in Lévi-Strauss and Sartre," *History and Theory* 10, no. 3 (1971): 290 ff.

26. Lévi-Strauss, "Réponses," 643.

27. Lévi-Strauss, "Le Temps du Mythe," 540.

28. Lévi-Strauss cited in Sanche de Gramont, "There are no Superior Societies," in *Claude Lévi-Strauss: The Anthropologist as Hero,* ed. E. Nelson and Tanya Hayes (Cambridge: MIT Press, 1970), 17.

29. *Ibid.,* 19.

30. Susan Sontag, "The Anthropologist as Hero," in her *Against Interpretation* (New York: Farrar Straus & Giroux, 1966), 196.

31. Claude Lévi-Strauss, *Race et histoire* (Paris: Gonthier, 1961), 85.

32. Simon Clarke, *The Foundations of Structuralism: A Critique of Lévi-Strauss and the Structuralist Movement* (New York: Harvester, 1981), 107.

33. Lévi-Strauss, "Réponses," 637.

34. Henri Lefebvre, "Claude Lévi-Strauss et le Nouvel Eléatisme," *L'Homme et la Société* 1 (1967): 31.

35. Lévi-Strauss, in *Sens et usages,* 150.

36. Claude Lévi-Strauss, *Tristes Tropiques* (Paris: Plon, 1955), 36.

37. *Ibid.,* 197.

38. Lévi-Strauss is also regarded as a transitional figure in leading French structuralism into semiotics. See Roland A. Champagne, "The Semiotics of Lévi-Strauss: Translation as Communication," in *The Semiotic Web—1989,* ed. Thomas A. Sebeok and Jean Ubiker-Sebeok (New York: Mouton de Gruyter, 1990), 1–25.

39. Paul Ricoeur, "Le Symbolisme et l'Explication Structurale," *Cahiers Internationaux de Symbolisme,* no. 1, 4 (1964): 88.

40. Bellour and Clément, *Claude Lévi-Strauss,* 166.

41. Catherine Backès-Clément, *Lévi-Strauss ou la structure du malheur* (Paris: Seghers, 1970), 7.

42. Claude Lévi-Strauss, *The Savage Mind* (Chicago: University of Chicago Press, 1966), 9.

Chapter Three

1. Susan Sontag in Roland Barthes, *A Barthes Reader,* ed. Susan Sontag (New York: Hill & Wang, 1982), xxii.

2. See Roland A. Champagne, *Beyond the Structuralist Myth of Écriture* (The Hague: Mouton, 1977), 82 ff., for a presentation of Barthes's elaboration of Sartre's prospectus in *Qu'est-ce que la littérature?*

3. Roland Barthes, *The Pleasure of the Text,* trans. Richard Miller (New York: Hill & Wang, 1975), 46.

4. Roland Barthes and Maurice Nadeau, *Sur la littérature* (Grenoble: Presses Universitaires de Grenoble, 1980), 23.

5. Interview with Roland Barthes, *VH101,* no. 1, 2 (Summer 1970): 11.

6. See Roland A. Champagne, *Literary History in the Wake of Roland Barthes* (Birmingham, Ala.: Summa, 1984), for a discussion of the prospectus for literary history by Barthes in contradistinction to the model offered by Lanson.

7. Roland Barthes, "The Death of the Author," in *Image Music Text,* trans. Stephen Heath (New York: Hill & Wang, 1977), 147.

8. Barthes, *A Barthes Reader,* 107.

9. Jonathan Culler, *Structuralist Poetics* (Ithaca, N.Y.: Cornell University Press, 1975), 54.

10. Sontag, "Writing Itself: On Roland Barthes," in *A Barthes Reader,* xxvii.

11. Roland Barthes, "Le Message Photographique," *Communications,* no. 1 (1961): 129: "Décrire, ce n'est donc pas seulement être inexact ou incomplet, c'est changer de structure, c'est signifier autre chose que ce qui est montré." ("Describing is not only being inexact or incomplete, it is changing structure, signifying something other than what is shown.")

12. Roland Barthes, "Aujourd'hui Michelet," *L'Arc*, no. 13, 52 (February 1973): 25 ff.

13. Roland Barthes, "Historical Discourse," trans. Peter Wexler, in *Structuralism: A Reader*, ed. Michael Lane (London: Jonathan Cape, 1970), 154.

14. Roland Barthes, "Réponses," *Tel Quel* 11, no. 47 (1971): 89.

15. See Roland A. Champagne, "The Metamorphoses of Proteus," in his *Beyond the Structuralist Myth of Écriture*, 115–31, for a discussion of *Sade Fourier Loyola* (1971) as narratives of language systems invented by the logothètes.

16. Roland Barthes, *Critical Essays*, trans. Richard Howard (Chicago: Northwestern University Press, 1972), 267.

17. Roland Barthes, "To Write: An Intransitive Verb?," in *The Structuralist Controversy*, ed. Richard Macksey and Eugenio Donato (Baltimore: Johns Hopkins University Press, 1970), 134–45.

18. Roland Barthes, "Myth Today," in *A Barthes Reader*, 116.

19. Roland Barthes, "Portrait du Sémiologue en Artiste," *Le Monde* (9–10 January 1977): 14.

20. Steven Ungar, *Roland Barthes: The Professor of Desire* (Lincoln: University of Nebraska Press, 1983), 54.

21. Roland Barthes, "L'Analyse Rhétorique," in *Littérature et société—Problèmes de méthodologie et sociologie de la littérature* (Brussels: Editions de l'Institut de Sociologie, 1967), 35.

22. Edmund White, "From Albert Camus to Roland Barthes," *New York Times Book Review* 87 (12 September 1982): 34.

23. Philip Thody, *Roland Barthes: A Conservative Estimate* (Atlantic Highlands, N.J.: Humanities Press, 1977), 68.

24. Henri Lefebvre, "Réflexions sur le Structuralisme et l'Histoire," *Cahiers Internationaux de Sociologie* 35 (1963): 4.

25. See Barthes's introductory lecture to the Collège de France, wherein he spoke about the struggle with language inherent in "Literature" because of "le jeu de mots dont elle [la Littérature] est le théâtre" (cf. Barthes, "Portrait du Sémiologue en Artiste," 14).

26. Roland Barthes, "The Death of the Author," in *Image Music Text*, trans. Stephen Heath (New York: Hill & Wang, 1977), 142.

27. Roland Barthes, "Sur André Gide et son Journal," *Magazine Littéraire* 9, no. 97 (1975): 27.

28. Roland Barthes, *Erté*, trans. William Weaver (Parma: Ricci, 1973): 40: "The meaningful point of departure in Erté is not Woman (she becomes nothing, except her own coiffure; she is simply the cipher of mythic femininity), it is the Letter."

29. Roland Barthes, "Par dessus l'Épaule," *Critique* 29, no. 318 (November 1973), 968.

30. Roland Barthes, "Musica Practica," *L'Arc* 10, no. 40 (February 1970): 17.

31. Roland Barthes, *Critique et vérité* (Paris: Seuil, 1966), 78–79.

32. Barthes, *The Pleasure of the Text*, 6.

33. Roland Barthes, *Incidents* (Paris: Seuil, 1987), 115.

34. Barthes already had intuitions of the importance of grounding human meaning during the period when he was writing "mythologies." In his thesis for the doctorat d'état, which he never completed, he wrote in 1957 that "human language is not merely the model of meaning but its grounding" (*Système de la Mode*, Paris: Seuil, 1967, 7).

35. Barthes, *The Pleasure of the Text*, 17.

36. See Roland A. Champagne, "Between Orpheus and Eurydice: Roland Barthes and the Historicity of Reading," *Clio* 8 (Summer 1979): 229–38, for a discussion of the physical connections between Michelet and history.

37. Ungar, *Roland Barthes*, 120.

38. See Roland A. Champagne, "The Task of Clotho Re-Defined: Roland Barthes's Tapestry of Literary History," *L'Esprit Créateur* 22 (Spring 1982): 35–47, for a discussion of Barthes's view of Plato's *Crito* and of Socrates as a point of departure for a new literary history.

39. Roland Barthes, "Lecture de Brillat-Savarin," in Brillat-Savarin, *Physiologie du goût* (Paris: Hermann, 1975), 12 ff.

40. Jonathan Culler, *Roland Barthes* (New York: Oxford University Press, 1983) 22.

41. Richard Miller, in Barthes, *The Pleasure of the Text*, viii.

42. Barthes, *A Barthes Reader*, 403.

Chapter Four

1. Jacques Lacan, *Écrits* (Paris: Seuil, 1966), 19–75. See also a partial translation into English in *Yale French Studies*, no. 48 (1973): 38–72.

2. Jacques Derrida, "Facteur de la Vérité, *Poétique* 21 (1975): 96–147. See also a partial translation into English in *Yale French Studies*, no. 52 (1975): 31–113.

3. Claude Lévi-Strauss, "The Effectiveness of Symbols," in *Structural Anthropology*, trans. C. Jacobson and B. Schoepf (New York: Basic, 1963), 202.

4. Barbara Johnson, "The Frame of Reference: Poe, Lacan, Derrida," in *Psychoanalysis and the Question of the Text*, ed. Geoffrey H. Hartman (Baltimore: Johns Hopkins University Press, 1978), 170.

5. Jacques Lacan, "Les Écrits Techniques de Freud," in his *Le Séminaire* 1 (Paris: Le Seuil, 1975), 90.

6. Jane Gallop, *Reading Lacan* (Ithaca: Cornell University Press, 1985), 46.

7. Jacques Lacan, Discussion in *The Structuralist Controversy*, ed. Richard Macksey and Eugenio Donato (Baltimore: The Johns Hopkins Press, 1972) 198.

8. Jacques Lacan, *Écrits: A Selection*, trans. Alan Sheridan (New York: Norton, 1977), 103.

9. Jean Laplanche and Serge Leclaire, students of Lacan, cite his proposal for "une nouvelle signification" (a new meaning) whereby language is understood as the practice of pinning down one signifier to another ("épingler un signifiant à un

signifiant*) without recourse to the signified or the referent. See their article "L'Inconscient," in *Les Temps Modernes* 16, no. 183 (July 1961): 112 ff.

10. Jacques Lacan, *The Four Fundamental Concepts of Psychoanalysis*, trans. Alan Sheridan (London: Hogarth, 1977), 200.

11. Ferdinand de Saussure, *Course in General Linguistics*, trans. and ed. Wade Baskin (New York: McGraw-Hill, 1966) 9.

12. Jacques Lacan, "Seminar on 'The Purloined Letter,'" trans. Jeffrey Mehlman, *Yale French Studies*, no. 48 (1973): 59.

13. Lacan, *Écrits*, 258.

14. *Ibid.*, 866.

15. Gallop, *Reading Lacan*, 20.

16. Catherine Clément, *The Lives and Legends of Jacques Lacan*, trans. Arthur Goldhammer (New York: Columbia University Press, 1983), 80.

17. Émile Benveniste, *Le Vocabulaire des institutions européennes*, 1 and 2 (Paris: Minuit, 1970).

18. Louis Althusser, "Philosophie et Sciences Humaines," *Revue de l'Enseignement Philosophique* 11 (June-July 1963): n. 14.

19. Lacan, *Four Fundamental Concepts*, 205.

20. *Ibid.*, 239.

21. Jacques Lacan, "Adresse du Jury d'Accueil de l'École Freudienne de Paris à l'Assemblée avant son Vote," *Scilicet* 1, no. 2–3 (1970): 120.

22. Anthony Wilden, *The Language of the Self* (Baltimore: Johns Hopkins University Press, 1980), 230.

23. For a survey of Lacan's influence on the "Psych et Po" French feminists, see Claire Duchen, *Feminism in France—From May '68 to Mitterand* (London: Routledge & Kegan Paul, 1986), 84–97.

24. Luce Irigaray, *Ce sexe qui n'en est pas un* (Paris: Minuit, 1977), 159.

25. Lacan, *Écrits*, 86.

26. David Paul Funt, "The Question of the Subject: Lacan and Psychoanalysis," *The Psychoanalytic Review* 60, no. 3 (Fall 1973): 396 ff.

27. For an application of the Lacanian model for discourse to reading literature, in this case a Balzac short story, see Roland A. Champagne, "The Architectural Pattern of a Literary Artifact: A Lacanian Reading of Balzac's 'Jésus-Christ en Flandre,'" *Studies in Short Fiction* 15 (Winter 1978): 49–54.

28. Lacan, *Écrits*, 11.

29. *Ibid.*, 273.

30. Richard Harland, *Superstructuralism: The Philosophy of Structuralism and Superstructuralism* (London: Methuen, 1987), 39.

31. Clément, *Lives and Legends*, 21.

32. Jacques Lacan, Preface to Anika Lemaire's *Jacques Lacan*, trans. David Macey (London: Routledge & Kegan Paul, 1977), viii.

33. See Stuart Schneiderman, *The Death of an Intellectual Hero* (Cambridge:

Harvard University Press, 1983), 118 ff., for a discussion of these contributions by Lacan to the working sessions of psychoanalysts.

34. Clément, *Lives and Legends,* 60.

35. Alice Cherki, "Pour une Mémoire," in *Retour à Lacan,* ed. Jacques Sédat (Paris: Fayard, 1981), 72.

36. Clément, *Lives and Legends,* 29.

37. See Jacqueline Rose and Juliet Mitchell, *Feminine Sexuality: Jacques Lacan and the École Freudienne* (New York: Pantheon, 1983), 40 ff., for a feminist discussion of Lacan's insights into the castration complex.

38. Julia Kristeva's early work (*Le Texte du roman,* 1970) was an application of structural linguistics; see Roland A. Champagne, "*Le Roman du texte:* A Response to Julia Kristeva's Reading of La Sale's *Petit Jehan de Saintré*," *Sub-Stance* 4 (Fall 1972): 125–33. Kristeva's work on Bakhtin, combined with her modified feminism, has led her into semiotics and psychoanalysis. The *chora,* as a preconscious memory of the mother, is postulated by her as a response to the symbolic's domination by the father in her *Revolution in Poetic Language,* trans. Margaret Waller (New York: Columbia University Press, 1984), 26 ff.

39. Sigmund Freud, *Selected Writings,* vol. 23, trans. Alex Strachey (London: Hogarth Press, 1975), 16.

40. Jacques Lacan, "Dieu et la Jouissance de la Femme," in his *Le Séminaire 20: Encore* (Paris: Seuil, 1975), 68.

41. Lacan, *Écrits,* 288.

42. Serge Leclaire, *Psychanalyser* (Paris: Seuil, 1968), 176.

43. Rose and Mitchell, *Feminine Sexuality,* 40.

44. Saussure, *Course,* 8.

45. Shoshana Felman, "To Open the Question," *Yale French Studies,* nos. 55–56 (1977): 7.

46. Cited by Leclaire, *Psychanalyser,* 181, n. 2.

47. Jacques Derrida, *La Carte Postale* (Paris: Flammarion, 1980), 457 ff.

48. Schneiderman, *Death,* 17.

49. As cited by Clément, *Lives and Legends,* 60.

Chapter Five

1. Fernand Braudel had exposed the limitations of this conception of history in May 1946, "What Paul Lacombe and François Simiand called 'l'histoire événementielle,' that is, the history of events: surface disturbances, crests of foam that the tides of history carry on their strong backs. . . . We must learn to distrust this history with its still burning passions, as it was felt, described, and lived by contemporaries whose lives were as short and as short-sighted as ours." (*The Mediterranean and the Mediterranean World in the Age of Philip II,* 1, trans. Sian Reynolds, New York: Harper & Row, 1972, 21).

2. *Ibid.,* 22.

3. Michel Foucault, *The Order of Things* (New York: Vintage, 1973), 374.

4. *Ibid.*, 385. I thank Father John Davis, O.P., of Providence College for leading me to a well-developed presentation of the "negative theology" implied by Foucault's reply to Nietzsche's "death of God" in James Bernauer, S.J., "The Prisons of Man," *International Philosophical Quarterly* 28, no. 4 (December 1987): 365–80.

5. Michel Foucault, *Language, Counter-Memory, Practice,* trans. Donald Bouchard and Sherry Simon (Ithaca: Cornell University Press, 1977), 221.

6. Karlis Racevski, *Michel Foucault and the Subversion of the Intellect* (Ithaca: Cornell University Press, 1983), 63.

7. Michel Foucault, "Monstrosities in Criticism," *Diacritics* 1 (Fall 1971): 60.

8. Michel Foucault, *The Archaeology of Knowledge,* trans. A. M. Sheridan Smith (New York: Random House & Pantheon, 1972), 235.

9. Hayden White, "Foucault Decoded: Notes from the Underground," in his *Tropics of Discourse* (Baltimore: Johns Hopkins University Press, 1978), 234.

10. Michel Foucault, *The Birth of the Clinic,* trans. A. M. Sheridan Smith (London: Pantheon, 1973), 31.

11. For a discussion of Blanchot's arguments for the gaze as a philosophical and literary device, see Roland A. Champagne, "A Mosaic View: The Poetics of Maurice Blanchot," *The Literary Review* 21 (Summer 1978): pp. 425–35.

12. Michel Foucault, in Lucette Finas, "Entretien avec Michel Foucault: Les Rapports de Pouvoir Passent à l'Intérieur des Corps," *Quinzaine littéraire,* no. 247 (1–15 January 1977), 5, speaks of his abandoned project for "a whole series of binary divisions, which in their own way would have reintroduced the great division 'reason-unreason' that I have tried to reconstitute with respect to insanity."

13. Hayden White has been the one English-speaking historian clearly sympathetic to Foucault's readings. Typically hostile are George Huppert's objection to the Renaissance according to Foucault ("*Divinatio* et *Eruditio*: Thoughts on Foucault," *History and Theory* 13 (1974): 191–207) and G. S. Rousseau's rejection of the Enlightenment in Foucault's eyes ("Whose Enlightenment? Not Man's: The Case of Michel Foucault," *Eighteenth Century Studies* 6, no. 2 (Fall 1972): 238–55).

14. Mikhail M. Bakhtin, *The Dialogic Imagination,* eds. Michael Holquist and Caryl Emerson (Austin: University of Texas Press, 1981), 426.

15. Richard Rorty, "Foucault and Epistemology," in *Foucault: A Critical Reader,* ed. David Couzens Hoy (London: Blackwell, 1986), 41.

16. Michel Foucault, *L'Ordre du discours* (Paris: Gallimard, 1971), 9.

17. Jean Piaget, *Structuralism,* trans. Chaninah Maschler (New York: Harper Torchbooks, 1979), 132.

18. Michel Foucault, *The History of Sexuality,* vol. 1, trans. Robert Hurley (New York: Pantheon, 1978), 93.

19. Jürgen Habermas (*Toward a Rational Society,* trans. Jeremy Shapiro, Boston: Beacon, 1970, 59) remarked that a critical intellectual, like a psychoanalyst relative to the analysand, has a responsibility to the public for undoing the repressive

effects of power. Hans-Georg Gadamer ("Replik," in *Hermeneutik und Ideo-logiekritik*, ed. Karl-Otto Apel, Frankfurt am Main: Klostermann, 1971, 294–95) replied that the stakes are very high because the intellectual risks anarchy against the tyranny of reason. Thus, the second generation of the Frankfurt School dramatized the dialectical struggle of power between the domination by an unknown institution on the one hand and by the tyranny of an enlightened observer on the other.

20. Michel Foucault, *Discipline and Punish—The Birth of the Prison*, trans. Allen Lane (London: Penguin, 1977), 26.

21. Piaget, *Structuralism*, 131.

22. Jean Baudrillard, *Forget Foucault*, trans. Nicole Dufresne (New York: Semiotexte, 1987), 10.

23. Foucault, *The Order of Things*, 117.

24. Hubert L. Dreyfus and Paul Rabinow, *Michel Foucault: Beyond Structuralism and Hermeneutics* (Chicago: Chicago University Press, 1982), viii.

25. Finas, "Entretien," 6.

26. Fredric Jameson, *The Political Unconscious* (Ithaca: Cornell University Press, 1981), 142. His colleague at Duke University, Frank Lentricchia, likewise chides Foucault (*Ariel and the Police*, Madison: University of Wisconsin Press, 1988, 48): "Foucault is wrong. His reading of resistant power as impervious metaphysical forces is belied by the history which he narrates."

27. Cited by François Ewald, "Anatomie et Corps Politique," *Critique* 31, no. 343 (December 1975): 1228.

28. Raymond Bellour, "Deuxième Entretien avec Michel Foucault," *Les Lettres Françaises*, no. 1187 (June 15–21, 1967), 8.

29. Michel Foucault, *Folie et déraison* (Paris: Gallimard, 1961), 40.

30. For a discussion of how Bataille narrated the repressive presence of capitalism, the Church, and fascism in his short story "L'Histoire de l'Oeil" (1928), see Roland A. Champagne, "The Parodic Dialogue of an Eye for an I in George Bataille's 'Story of the Eye,'" in *Whimsy 6: International Humor*, ed. Don and Alleen Nilsen (Tempe: Arizona State University Press, 1988), 193–95.

31. Michel Foucault, *Mental Illness and Psychology*, trans. Alan Sheridan (New York: Random House/Pantheon, 1976), 75.

32. Ferdinando Scianna, "La Nuova Sessualità: Rivoluzionaria Analisi del Nuovo Sartre," *L'Europeo* (18 February 1977): 49–53.

33. Barthes, "Taking Sides," in his *Critical Essays*, trans. Richard Howard (Chicago: Northwestern University Press, 1972), 170.

34. Michel Foucault, *This Is Not a Pipe*, trans. James Harkness (Berkeley: University of California Press, 1983), 54.

35. Michel Foucault, "Prison Walk," trans. Colin Gordon, in *Radical Philosophy Reader*, ed. Richard Osborne (London: Verso, 1985), 15.

36. Foucault, *Language*, 139.

37. Peter L. Berger and Thomas Luckmann, *The Social Construction of Reality* (New York: Anchor, 1966), 60.

38. Foucault, *History of Sexuality,* 37.

39. Georges Canguilhem, "Mort de l'Honneur ou Épuisement du Cogito?" *Critique* 23 no. 242 (July 1967): 600.

40. Foucault, *Language,* 153.

41. Foucault, *History of Sexuality,* 37.

42. *Ibid.,* 5.

43. Barthes, "Taking Sides," 170.

44. See the interview with Bernard-Henri Lévy in which Foucault presents how the religious ritual of confession unlocked the sexual misery of Christians, in "Power and Sex," trans. David J. Parent, *Telos* 10, no. 32 (Summer 1977): 152–61.

45. Michel Foucault, "Firm and Popular Memory," trans. Martin Jordan, *Radical Philosophy,* no. 11 (Summer 1975): 25–26.

46. Foucault, *History of Sexuality,* 159.

47. Gilles Deleuze, "Ecrivain Non: Un Nouveau Cartographe," *Critique,* no. 31 (1975): 1210 ff. See his revised, translated version "A New Cartographer," in his *Foucault,* trans. Sean Hand (Minneapolis: University of Minnesota Press, 1988), 23–44.

48. Richard Harland, *Superstructuralism: The Philosophy of Structuralism and Superstructuralism* (London: Methuen, 1987), 102.

49. Paul Roth, "Who Needs Paradigms?" *Metaphilosophy* 15, no. 3–4 (July/October 1984): 230.

50. Foucault, *Language,* 208.

51. Foucault, *History of Sexuality,* 93.

52. Baudrillard, Interview with Sylvère Lotringer, in his *Forget Foucault,* 68.

53. *Ibid.,* 43.

Chapter Six

1. Edith Kurzweil, *The Age of Structuralism: Lévi-Strauss to Foucault* (New York: Columbia University Press, 1980), 40.

2. Miriam Glucksmann, *Structuralist Analysis in Contemporary Social Thought* (London: Routledge & Kegan Paul, 1974), 149.

3. Catherine Clément, *The Lives and Legends of Jacques Lacan,* trans. Arthur Goldhammer (New York: Columbia University Press, 1983), 21.

4. Louis Althusser, letter to Ben Brewster, in his *For Marx,* trans. Ben Brewster (New York: Vintage Books, 1970), 257.

5. Louis Althusser, *Pour Marx* (Paris: Maspero, 1965), 238.

6. Louis Althusser, *Essays in Self-Criticism,* trans. Ben Brewster (London: New Left Books, 1976), 51.

7. See Miriam Glucksmann, *Structuralist Analysis,* 170 ff., for a discussion of their debate.

8. *Ibid.,* 85.

9. Louis Althusser and E. Balibar, *Reading Capital,* trans. Ben Brewster (London: New Left Books, 1970), 180.

10. Louis Althusser, "Marx's Immense Theoretical Revolution," in *The Structuralists from Marx to Lévi-Strauss*, ed. Richard and Fernande De George (Garden City: Anchor Books, 1972), 239.

11. Althusser, *For Marx*, 32.

12. Henri Lefebvre, *Structuralisme et marxisme* (Paris: U.G.E., 1970), 95.

13. Althusser, "Theoretical Revolution," 249.

14. Louis Althusser and E. Balibar, *Lire le Capital*, v. 1, (Paris: Maspero, 1965), x.

15. Althusser, *For Marx*, 192.

16. Edgar P. Thompson, *The Poverty of Theory and Other Essays* (New York and London: Monthly Review Press, 1978), 106.

17. Louis Althusser, *Réponse à John Lewis* (Paris: Maspero, 1973), 54.

18. Althusser, *Reading Capital*, 59.

19. Althusser, *For Marx*, 205, n. 44.

20. Althusser, *Réponse à John Lewis*, 67.

21. Alex Callinicos, *Althusser's Marxism* (London: Pluto Press, 1976), 101.

22. Thompson, *Poverty of Theory*, 9.

23. Raymond Aron, *D'une sainte famille à l'autre* (Paris: Gallimard, 1970), 8–9.

24. *Ibid.*, 105.

25. Althusser, *Pour Marx*, 238.

26. Althusser, *Reading Capital*, 17.

27. André Glucksmann, "Un Structuralisme Ventriloque," *Les Temps Modernes* 22, no. 250 (March 1967): 1584.

28. Richard Harlan, *Superstructuralism: The Philosophy of Structuralism and Superstructuralism* (London: Methuen, 1987), 100.

29. André Glucksmann, "Un Structuralisme Ventriloque," 1598.

30. Jean Piaget, *Structuralism,* trans. Chaninah Maschler (New York: Harper Torchbooks, 1979), 126.

31. Althusser, *For Marx*, 256.

32. Jean-Pierre Cotten, *La Pensée de Louis Althusser* (Paris: Privat, 1979), 125.

33. Henri Lefebvre, *Au-delà du structuralisme* (Paris: Anthropos, 1971), 353.

34. Althusser, *For Marx*, 173.

35. Jacques Rancière, *La Leçon d'Althusser* (Paris: Gallimard, 1974), 209.

36. Louis Althusser, *Ce qui ne peut plus durer dans le parti communiste* (Paris: Maspero, 1978), 17–19.

37. *Ibid.*, 30.

Chapter Seven

1. Louis Althusser, *Pour Marx* (Paris, Maspero, 1965), 121.

2. Karl Marx, "Thèses sur Feuerbach," in his and Friedrich Engels's

L'Idéologie allemande, trans. Renée Cartelle and Gilbert Badia (Paris: Éditions Sociales, 1968), 56.

3. Michel Foucault, Preface to Gilles Deleuze and Félix Guattari, *Anti-Oedipus: Capitalism and Schizophrenia,* trans. Robert Hurley et al. (New York: Viking Press, 1977), xiv.

4. Annie Cohen-Solal, *Sartre—A Life,* trans. Anna Cancogni (New York: Pantheon, 1987), 451.

5. Claude Lévi-Strauss, *Tristes Tropiques,* (Paris: Plon, 1955), 197.

6. Examples of their pronouncements about the "death of man" include, but are not limited to, the following statement. Althusser (*For Marx,* 229): "It is impossible to know anything about man except on the absolute precondition that the philosophical (theoretical) myth of man is reduced to ashes"; Foucault (*The Order of Things,* 385): "Rather than the death of God . . . what Nietzsche's thought heralds is the death of his murderer"; Lévi-Strauss (*The Savage Mind,* 247): "I believe the ultimate goal of the human sciences to be not to constitute, but to dissolve man."

7. André Glucksmann, *The Master Thinkers,* trans. Brian Pearce (New York: Harper and Row, 1980), 118.

8. Gilles Deleuze, *Foucault,* trans. Sean Hand (Minneapolis: University of Minnesota Press, 1988), 30.

9. Hubert Cambrier and Philippe Fraschira, *Pour une pratique marxiste de la philosophie* (Brussels: Fondation Joseph Jacquemotte & Contradictions, 1983), 138.

10. See Roland A. Champagne, "Prometheus Measuring the Universe: Michel Serres's Semiotic-Reading Model in the Wake of Structuralism," *Semiotic Scene* 1, no. 2 (April 1977): 39–48, for a discussion of the thermodynamics of Gassendi and Cyrano de Bergerac as revealed by Serres's logoanalysis.

11. Michel Serres, *Hermes II—L'Interférence* (Paris: Minuit, 1972), 12.

12. *Ibid.,* 9.

13. André Martinet, *Elements of General Linguistics,* trans. L. R. Palmer (Chicago: University of Chicago Press, 1964), 24.

14. Émile Benveniste, *Problems in General Linguistics,* trans. Mary Elizabeth Meek (Coral Gables, Fla.: University of Miami Press, 1971), 24.

15. Glucksmann, *The Master Thinkers,* 120.

16. *Ibid.,* 210.

17. Christian Jambet and Guy Lardreau, *L'Ange—Pour une cynégétique du semblant* (Paris: Grasset, 1976), 30.

18. See Roland A. Champagne, "Revealing the Ideological Mask of Culture: The French New Philosophers, Maupassant, and Literary Criticism," *Language and Style* 18 (Winter 85–86): 232–41, for the application of "angelic discourse" to the analysis of a literary document.

19. Maurice Clavel, in *Délivrance face à face,* ed. Jacques Paugam (Paris: Seuil, 1977), 28 ff.

20. Bernard-Henri Lévy, "Le Vrai Crime de Soljenitsyne," *Le Nouvel Observateur* (30 June 1975): 54 ff.

21. Deleuze, *Foucault,* 107 ff.

22. Martin Heidegger, *On the Way to Language,* trans. Peter D. Hertz (New York: Harper & Row, 1971), 40.

23. Deleuze, *Foucault,* 22.

24. An example of the use of the double helix to explain gender issues can be found in *Behind the Lines,* ed. Margaret R. Higonnet et al. (New Haven: Yale University Press, 1987), which discusses gender issues between the two world wars. Her essay, "Double Helix," provides inspiration for other contributors to apply the image to expose additional hidden problems with gender folds.

25. Michel Serres, *Le système de Leibniz et ses modèles mathématiques,* 1 (Paris: Presses Universitaires de France, 1968), 30.

26. Michel Foucault, *Language, Counter-Memory, Practice,* trans. Donald Bouchard and Sherry Simon (Ithaca: Cornell University Press, 1977), 165.

27. See Roland A. Champagne, "Words Disguising Desire: Serial Discourse and the Dual Character of Suzanne Simonin," *Kentucky Romance Quarterly* 28 (Winter 1981–82): 341–50, for a discussion of the series as a tool for explaining narrative order. The "indeterminate factor" is especially helpful in analyzing a story with several narratives hidden beneath the surface as in Diderot's *La Religieuse.*

28. Gilles Deleuze, *Logique du sens* (Paris: Minuit, 1969), 92.

29. See Roland A. Champagne, "A Schizoanalysis of Marcel: Gilles Deleuze's Critical Theories at Work," *Helicon* (Ohio State University), no. 2 (Spring 1975): 39–50, for a discussion of Marcel Proust as a "desiring machine" in the spirit of Deleuze and Guattari.

30. Gilles Deleuze, "Schizologie," in Louis Wolfson, *Le Schizo et les langues* (Paris: Gallimard, 1970), 23.

31. Michel Serres, "Ce qui est écrit dans le code," *Critique* 27, no. 290 (July 1971): 585.

32. Serres, *Hermes II,* 71.

33. *Ibid.,* 17.

34. Deleuze, *Foucault,* 132.

Chapter Eight

1. Roman Jakobson, "Linguistics and Poetics," in *Style in Language,* ed. Thomas A. Sebeok (Cambridge: MIT Press, 1960), 353 ff.

2. Tzvetan Todorov, *Grammaire du Décaméron* (The Hague: Mouton, 1969), 15 ff.

3. For a more extended presentation of the French contextualist school of classical mythology, see Roland A. Champagne, *The Structuralists on Myth: The Vernant Group of Contextual Analysis* (New York: Garland Publications), to appear in 1992.

4. Jean Dubois, *La Grammaire structurale du français,* 1 (Paris: Larousse, 1965), 85.

5. Noam Chomsky, *Syntactic Structures* (The Hague: Mouton, 1965), 17.

6. Jean Dubois, "Pourquoi des Dictionnaires?" *Social Science Information* 6, no. 4 (1967): 102.

7. Nicolas Ruwet, "Rhétorique et Herméneutique," *Poétique,* no. 23 (1975): 371 ff.

8. For individual insights into these works, see the book reviews by Roland A. Champagne of *Maupassant* (*The French Review,* February 1977, 501–502); *Sémiotique et sciences sociales* (*World Literature Today,* Spring 1977, 249); *Semiotics and Language* (*Modern Language Journal,* Autumn 1984, 299–300); and *Structural Semantics* (*World Literature Today,* Summer 1984, 482).

9. A. J. Greimas, *Maupassant: La sémiotique du texte* (Paris: Le Seuil, 1976), 228.

10. Ronald Schleifer, *A. J. Greimas and the Nature of Meaning* (Lincoln: University of Nebraska Press, 1987), 57 ff.

11. Greimas, *Maupassant,* 167.

12. Fredric Jameson, *The Prison-House of Language* (Princeton: Princeton University Press, 1972), 216.

13. The testimonies given to Greimas upon his retirement are noteworthy because of the wide range of intellectuals he has influenced and who will continue his work. Solomon Marcus (Bucharest), Paul Zumthor (Montreal), Louis Marin (Paris-X), and Umberto Eco (Bologna) are just some of the contributors. See the festschrift edited by Herman Parret and Hans-George Ruprecht in two volumes entitled *Exigences et perspectives de la sémiotique* (Amsterdam: Benjamins, 1985).

14. Schleifer, *Greimas,* 34.

15. Roland Barthes, "To Write: An Intransitive Verb?" in *The Structuralist Controversy,* ed. Richard Macksey and Eugenio Donato (Baltimore: Johns Hopkins University Press, 1970), 134–45.

16. Tzvetan Todorov, *Théories du symbole* (Paris: Seuil, 1977), 85.

17. See Roland A. Champagne, "The New Rhetoric: A Dialectical Prospectus for the Future," *Delta Epsilon Sigma Bulletin* 24, no. 4 (December 1979): 115–120, for a discussion of the classical rhetorical schools as forerunners of the structuralist new rhetoric.

18. Émile Benveniste, "De la Subjectivité dans le Langage," *Journal de Psychologie* 55 (1958): 257–65. See chapter 21 of his *Problems in General Linguistics* for a translation of this essay.

19. Barbara Herrnstein Smith, *On the Margins of Discourse* (Chicago: University of Chicago Press, 1978), 85.

20. Maurice Blanchot, *L'Entretien infini* (Paris: Gallimard, 1969), 500.

21. See Roland A. Champagne, "A Mosaic View: The Poetics of Maurice Blanchot," *The Literary Review* 21 (Summer 1978): 425–35, for a discussion of Blanchot as a seer-like Moses leading the blind in the desert and unable himself ever to see the Promised Land.

22. Jacques Derrida, *De la Grammatologie* (Paris: Minuit, 1967), 378.

23. Hayden White, *Tropics of Discourse* (Baltimore: Johns Hopkins University Press, 1978), 252.

24. Paul de Man, "Semiology and Rhetoric," *Diacritics* 3, no. 3 (Fall 1973): 30.

25. Gérard Genette, *Figures III* (Paris: Seuil, 1972), 23.

26. For example, in their *Rhetorique générale* (Paris: Larousse, 1970), Group μ noted: "In a language without any semantic redundance, where blocks of meaning follow each other like prayer beads, no (semantic) figure of speech would be possible" (p. 96). Thus, for them, the metaphor, by expressly setting up the links between disparate objects, is the chief figure of speech in a grammar presenting the clarity of the French language when it is properly used.

27. I have borrowed Jane F. Lewin's terms for the French as she translated Gérard Genette's *Narrative Discourse* (Ithaca: Cornell University Press, 1980), 27.

28. Genette, *Figures III, 243.

29. Vladimir Propp, *Morphology of the Folktale,* trans. Laurence Scott (Austin: University of Texas Press, 1968), 21.

30. Claude Bremond, "Morphology of the French Folktale," *Semiotica* 11, no. 3 (1970): 256.

31. Jonathan Culler, *Structuralist Poetics* (Ithaca, N.Y.: Cornell University Press, 1975), 209.

32. Claude Bremond, "La Logique des Possibles Narratifs," *Communications,* no. 8 (1966): 76.

33. Claude Bremond, *Logique du récit* (Paris: Seuil, 1973), 321.

34. Roland Barthes, "Introduction à l'Analyse Structurale du Récit," *Communications,* no. 8 (1966): 25 ff.

35. See Roland A. Champagne, "The Spiralling *Discours:* Todorov's Model for a Narratology," *L'Esprit Créateur* 14, no. 4 (Winter 1974): 342–53, for Todorov's method applied to Laclos's *Les Liaisons dangereuses* (1782).

36. Tzvetan Todorov, "The Origin of Genres," *New Literary History* 8, no. 1 (Autumn 1976): 163.

37. See, for example, the exploration of the comic theories of Bakhtin for gender roles in narratives in Roland A. Champagne's "The Engendered Blow Job: Bakhtin's Comic Dismemberment and the Pornography of Georges Bataille's 'Story of the Eye,'" *Humor: International Journal of Humor Research* 3 (1990): 177–191.

38. Todorov, *Théories du symbole,* 358.

39. Jurij Lotman, "Different Cultures, Different Codes," *Times Literary Supplement,* no. 3736 (12 October 1973): 1213.

40. Philippe Hamon, "Text and Ideology: For a Poetics of the Norm," *Style* 17, no. 2 (Spring 1983): 95.

41. The influence of narratology is spreading into the analysis of many components of culture other than traditional prose stories. For example, Nina Claire Ekstein has applied the principles of narratology to identify narratives within

seventeenth-century drama (e.g., her *Dramatic Narrative: Racine's Récits,* New York: Peter Lang, 1986) and how they function therein as dramatic techniques.

42. Tzvetan Todorov, *The Poetics of Prose,* trans. Richard Howard (Ithaca: Cornell University Press, 1977), 142.

43. Edgar Allan Poe, "The Purloined Letter," in *The Purloined Poe,* ed. J. P. Muller and W. J. Richardson (Baltimore: Johns Hopkins University Press, 1988), 18.

44. Jean-Pierre Vernant, *Myth and Society in Ancient Greece,* trans. Janet Lloyd (London and Atlantic Highlands: Harvester Press and Humanities Press, 1980), 229.

45. Claude Lévi-Strauss, "The Story of Asdiwal," in his *Structural Anthopology,* vol. 2, trans. Monique Layton (New York: Basic Books, 1976), 146–97.

46. Nicole Loraux, *The Invention of Athens: The Funeral Oration in the Classical City,* trans. Alan Sheridan (Cambridge: Harvard University Press, 1986), vii.

47. Marcel Detienne, "The Myth of 'Honeyed Orpheus,'" in *Myth, Religion and Society,* ed. R. L. Gordon (Cambridge: Cambridge University Press, 1981), 108.

48. Jean-François Lyotard, *La Condition Postmoderne* (Paris: Minuit, 1979), 41.

Chapter Nine

1. Michel Foucault, *Foucault/Blanchot,* ed. and trans. Brian Massumi and Jeffrey Mehlman (New York: Zone Books, 1987), 12–13.

2. Jean Piaget in *Conversations with Jean Piaget,* ed. Jean-Claude Bringuier, trans. Basia Miller Gulati (Chicago: University of Chicago Press, 1980), 18.

3. *Ibid.,* 3.

4. Ferdinand de Saussure, *Course in General Linguistics,* trans. Wade Baskin (New York: Harper Torchbooks, 1979), 16.

5. See Roland A. Champagne, "Anti-Structuralist Structures: The Avant-Garde Struggles of French Fiction," *Studies in Twentieth Century Literature,* 1 (Spring 1977): 135–55, for a discussion of Piaget's principles of structuralism as points of reference for exploring new aesthetics in contemporary French fiction.

6. Lucien Goldmann, "Structuralisme, Marxisme, Existentialisme," *L'Homme et la Société* 2 (1966): 109.

7. René Girard, *"To Double Business Bound"* (Baltimore: Johns Hopkins University Press, 1978), 216.

8. *Conversations with Piaget,* 13.

9. Jacques Lacan, *The Four Fundamental Concepts of Psychoanalysis,* trans. Alan Sheridan (London: Hogarth, 1977), 205.

10. For a discussion of the Erlanger Program of geometry, see Felix Klein, *Elementary Mathematics from an Advanced Viewpoint: Geometry,* trans. E. R. Hedrick and C. A. Noble (New York: Dover, 1939).

11. Jean Piaget in *Entretiens sur la notion de genèse et de structure,* ed. M. de Gandillac, L. Goldmann, and J. Piaget (The Hague: Mouton, 1965), 56.

12. Jean Piaget, *Structuralism,* trans. Chaninah Maschler (New York: Harper Torchbooks, 1979), 34.

13. See *Jean Piaget—Consensus and Controversy,* ed. Sohan Modgil and Celia Modgil (New York: Praeger, 1982), especially the editors' introduction, for an assessment by psychologists of the validity of Piaget's theory.

14. Piaget, *Structuralism,* 119.

15. Lucien Goldmann, *The Human Sciences and Philosophy,* trans. Hayden White and Robert Anchor (London: Jonathan Cape, 1964), 85–86.

16. Lucien Goldmann, *Essays on Method in the Sociology of Literature,* trans. William R. Boelhower (St. Louis: Telos Press, 1980), 96.

17. Lucien Goldmann, in *The Structuralist Controversy,* ed. Richard Macksey and Eugenio Donato (Baltimore: Johns Hopkins Press, 1972), 109.

18. Georg Lukács, *History and Class Consciousness,* trans. Rodney Livingstone (London: Merlin Press, 1971), 27.

19. Jean Hippolite, in *The Structuralist Controversy,* 111.

20. Lucien Goldmann, *Littérature et société* (Brussels: Éditions de l'Institut de Sociologie, 1967), 203.

21. Goldmann, in *The Structuralist Controversy,* 98.

22. Fredric Jameson, *The Ideologies of Theory,* vol. 1 (Minneapolis: University of Minnesota Press, 1988), 142 ff.

23. Serge Doubrovsky, *Pourquoi la nouvelle critique?* (Paris: Gonthier, 1972), 159.

24. Lucien Goldmann, "The Epistemology of Sociology," *Telos* 10, no. 30 (Winter 1976–77): 201.

25. Miriam Glucksmann, "Lucien Goldmann: Humanist or Marxist?" *New Left Review,* no. 56 (1969): 61.

26. Terry Eagleton, *Marxism and Literary Criticism* (Berkeley: University of California Press, 1976), 34.

27. Goldmann, in *Entretiens,* 55.

28. René Girard, in *Violent Origins,* ed. Robert G. Hamerton-Kelly (Stanford: Stanford University Press, 1987), 106.

29. René Girard, *The Violence and the Sacred,* trans. Patrick Gregory (Baltimore: Johns Hopkins University Press, 1977), 318.

30. René Girard, *Deceit, Desire, and the Novel,* trans. Yvonne Freccero (Baltimore: Johns Hopkins University Press, 1965), 2.

31. René Girard, "An Interview," Diacritics 8 (Spring 1978): 203.

32. Burton Mack, in *Violent Origins,* 10.

33. René Girard, *The Scapegoat,* trans. Yvonne Freccero (Baltimore: Johns Hopkins University Press, 1986), 11.

34. René Girard, "Generative Scapegoating," in *Violent Origins,* 92.

35. Girard, *"To double business bound,"* 166.

Chapter Ten

1. Roland Barthes, "The Structuralist Activity," in his *Critical Essays,* trans. Richard Howard (Chicago: Northwestern University Press, 1972), 213–20.

2. Claude Lévi-Strauss, in his and Didier Eribon's *De Près et de loin* (Paris: Odile Jacob, 1988), 105 ff.

3. Barthes, *Critical Essays,* 214.

4. Roland Barthes, "Par où commencer," *Poétique,* no. 1 (1970): 9.

5. See Peter Dews's discussion of this assumption as he compared Lacan and Habermas in *Logics of Disintegration* (London: Verso, 1987), 234 ff.

6. Roland Barthes, "Les Sciences Humaines et l'Oeuvre de Lévi-Strauss," *Annales* 19, no. 6 (December 1964): 1086.

7. Michel Foucault, *Foucault/Blanchot,* trans. Brian Mussumi and Jeffrey Mehlman (New York: Zone Books, 1987), 94.

8. Jean Baudrillard, *L'Effet Beaubourg* (Paris: Galilée, 1977), 9–10.

9. A. J. Greimas, *De l'imperfection* (Paris: Pierre Fanlac, 1987), 99.

10. Dews, *Logics,* 224.

11. John K. Sheriff, *The Fate of Meaning—Charles Peirce, Structuralism, and Literature* (Princeton: Princeton University Press, 1989), 140.

12. See Roland A. Champagne, "Semiotic Directions for Modern Fiction," *Dispositio* 3, no. 7–8 (Winter 1978): 85–102.

Annotated Bibliography

PRIMARY WORKS

Books

Althusser, Louis. *For Marx*. Trans. Ben Brewster. London: Penguin, 1969. Includes a glossary of Althusser's terms and a letter from him refuting "Althusserianism."

Baran, Henryk, ed. *Semiotics and Structuralism*. White Plains: International Arts and Sciences Press, 1976. Anthology of Soviet scholars struggling with methods; Lotman's essays (6) are noteworthy.

Barthes, Roland. *A Barthes Reader*. Ed. Susan Sontag. New York: Hill & Wang, 1982. Best of Barthes's essays translated into English. Richard Howard's translation of Barthes's inaugural lecture to the Collège de France on literary semiology is especially remarkable.

Foucault, Michel. *Power/Knowledge*. Ed. and trans. Colin Gordon et al. New York: Pantheon, 1980. Interviews and essays by Foucault on this topic; bibliography of Foucault's writings up to June 1979.

Glucksmann, André. *The Master Thinkers*. Trans. Brian Pearce. New York: Harper & Row, 1980. A basic text of the French New Philosophers.

Gordon, R. L., ed. *Myth, Religion and Society*. Cambridge: Cambridge University Press, 1981. Representative essays of the Vernant contextualist group of structural mythological studies by Jean-Pierre Vernant, Marcel Detienne, Pierre Vidal-Naquet, and Louis Gernet.

Greimas, A. J. *On Meaning*. Trans. Paul J. Perron and Frank H. Collins. Minneapolis: University of Minnesota Press, 1987. Representative essays from various books by Greimas; foreword by Fredric Jameson.

Lévi-Strauss, Claude. *Anthropology and Myth*. Trans. Roy Willis. London: Basil Blackwell, 1984. His notes to his lectures from 1951 to 1982 given at the Collège de France; bases for most of his articles and books; useful index.

Matejka, Ladislav, and Krystyna Pomorska, ed. *Readings in Russian Poetics: Formalist and Structuralist Views*. Cambridge, Mass.: MIT Press, 1971. Representative anthology of formalists from the 1920s and 1930s; Eichenbaum's "The Theory of the Formal Method" is informative.

Muller, John P., and William J. Richardson, ed. *The Purloined Poe*. Baltimore: Johns Hopkins University Press, 1988. Poe's short story "The Purloined Letter," Lacan's seminar on the story, replies by Derrida, Johnson, Gallop, and Harvey to Lacan, and other readings of the story.

Piaget, Jean. *Structuralism*. Trans. Chaninah Maschler. New York: Basic Books, 1970. Contributions of the sciences to the definition of *structuralism*.

Saussure, Ferdinand de. *Cours de linguistique générale*. Ed. Rudolf Engler. Wiesbaden: Harassowit, 1967. Critical edition with student notes from which Bally and Sechehaye constructed the text. English translation of original edition by Bally, Sechehaye, and Riedlinger published as *Course in General Linguistics*, trans. Wade Baskin, New York: McGraw-Hill, 1966.

Steiner, Peter, ed. *The Prague School*. Austin: University of Texas Press, 1982. Arts, folklore, and linguistics of Steiner, which is presented not merely as a transition from formalism to structuralism.

Todorov, Tzvetan. *Introduction to Poetics*. Trans. Richard Howard. Minneapolis: University of Minnesota Press, 1981. Originally published as *What Is Structuralism?* in French; clear presentation of the stakes of poetics and narratology.

Journal

Barthes, Roland, ed. Special issue (no. 8) of *Communications* on the Structural Analysis of Narrative. Paris: École Pratique des Hautes Études, 1966. Seminal articles by Barthes, Claude Bremond, Tzvetan Todorov, Christian Metz, and Gérard Genette.

Bibliographies

Bernauer, James, and Thomas Keenan. "The Works of Michel Foucault," in *The Final Foucault,* ed. James Bernauer and David Rasmussen (Cambridge: MIT Press, 1988), 119–58. Chronological order of composition; includes all English studies directed by Foucault.

Clark, Michael. *Michel Foucault: An Annotated Bibliography*. New York: Garland, 1983. Useful, but does not include *Désordre de la famille* (1982) and later works by Foucault; first entry of 1952 thesis does not belong to this Foucault.

Harari, Josué V. *Structuralists and Structuralisms*. Ithaca: Diacritics, 1971. French contemporary thought from 1960 to 1970.

Miller, Joan M. *French Structuralism: A Multidisciplinary Bibliography*. New York: Garland, 1981. Period 1968–78; Summer 1980 is latest entry; application by discipline; very few critical annotations; primary, secondary, and book review references.

SECONDARY WORKS

Books

Callinicos, Alex. *Althusser's Marxism*. London: Pluto Press, 1976. Althusser's position cannot be held by a consistent revolutionary. Althusser's politics and philosophy are at odds with each other.

Cambier, Hubert, and Philippe Fraschira. *Pour une pratique marxiste de la philosophie.* Brussels: F. J. Jacquemotte and Contradictions, 1983. Althusser-inspired prospectus of philosophy; explanation and defense of Althusser's Marxism.

Clément, Catherine. *The Lives and Legends of Jacques Lacan.* Trans. Arthur Goldhammer. New York: Columbia University Press, 1983. Important biographical information on Lacan by a convert to his style; not chonologically ordered; appreciation from within Lacan's "philosophy."

Culler, Jonathan. *Ferdinand de Saussure.* London: Fontana, 1976. Based on Engler's critical edition of Saussure; what Saussure really thought rather than what Bally et al. presented in 1916.

————. *Structuralist Poetics.* Ithaca: Cornell University Press, 1975. Doctorate of Philosophy thesis, Oxford University; Chomsky's "performance" as a criterion for structuralism; Barthes and Lévi-Strauss misunderstood linguistics; Culler's well-digested readings of structuralists form the basis for a "poetics."

Doubrovsky, Serge, ed. *The New Criticism in France.* Trans. Derek Coltman. Chicago: Chicago University Press, 1973. Barthes/Picard debates as a showcase for a renewal of literary criticism.

Duchen, Claire. *Feminism in France: May '68 to Mitterand.* London: Routledge & Kegan Paul, 1986. Survey of the "Psych et Po" domination of the French feminist movement; based on theories by Lacan, Foucault, and Derrida.

Glucksmann, Miriam. *Structuralist Analysis in Contemporary Social Thought.* London: Routledge & Kegan Paul, 1974. Doctoral thesis, University of London; comparison of theories by Lévi-Strauss and Althusser; thorough presentation of their predecessors.

Jameson, Fredric. *The Prison-House of Language: A Critical Account of Structuralism and Russian Formalism.* Princeton: Princeton University Press, 1972. The "critical" values are the dialectic, materialism, historicity, and Marxism.

Johnson, Barbara. *The Critical Difference.* Baltimore: Johns Hopkins University Press, 1980. Reading of Barthes's *S/Z* as an example of criticism as literature. Incisive presentation of Barthes's work as Derridean in spirit.

Lemert, Charles C., and Garth Gillian. *Michel Foucault: Social Theory and Transgression.* New York: Columbia University Press, 1982. Insightful presentation on Foucault by topics; glossary of his terms in appendix; limited by date; overview of his contributions to the understanding of history.

Macksey, Richard, and Eugenio Donato, ed. *The Structuralist Controversy: The Languages of Criticism and the Sciences of Man.* Baltimore: Johns Hopkins University Press, 1972. Proceedings of the 1966 seminar at Johns Hopkins University; Todorov, Barthes, Lacan, Derrida, Goldmann, and Ruwet gave remarkable lectures; discussions with René Girard, Georges Poulet, and Charles Morazé were spirited.

Mitchell, Juliet, and Jacqueline Rose. *Feminine Sexuality: Jacques Lacan and the École Freudienne.* New York: Pantheon, 1983. Lacan's challenge to traditional psychoanalytic theories; centrality of the castration complex in ascribing sexual roles to men and women.

Muller, John P., and William J. Richardson. *Lacan and Language: A Reader's Guide to "Écrits."* New York: International Universities, 1982. English translation of Lacan's earliest essays; introduction is a clear overview of Lacan's writings within the context of psychoanalysis, Lévi-Strauss, and structural linguistics; map and notes for nine of Lacan's major essays.

Smith, Steven B. *Reading Althusser.* Ithaca: Cornell University Press, 1984. "Humanistic context" of Althusser; dismisses E. P. Thompson's outrage at Althusser with a defense of the historian's craft.

Ungar, Steven. *Roland Barthes: The Professor of Desire.* Lincoln: University of Nebraska Press, 1983. Barthes's evolving obsession with his physical body helps us to understand his work as a book of love.

Article

Benoist, Jean-Marie. "Structuralism: A New Frontier." *The Cambridge Review,* 22 October 1971, 10–17. Piaget's structuralism as an improvement on Chomsky's innate ideas. Piaget's "revolution" focused on the equilibrium of the epistemic subject.

Index

Humanism, 27, 30, 51, 61, 62, 76,
78, 80, 81, 82, 90, 129
Humanitarian, 29, 30
Humanities, 3, 4, 18, 20
Human sciences, 23, 27, 60, 61, 64, 65,
104, 109
Human spirit, 16, 17, 21–31, 91, 122, 123
Hypnosis, 49, 55–56, 126
Hyppolite, Jean, 116

Idealism, 31, 61
Ideologists, 19, 32, 33, 47, 62, 75, 77,
78, 88, 89, 90, 91, 122–124
Ideology, 2, 3, 5, 6–7, 19, 30, 33, 36, 37,
40, 45–46, 48, 59, 75–87, 89, 90,
108, 110, 112, 116, 122–124
Illness, 60–74
Imaginary, 35, 48, 53, 54
Incarceration, 60–74
Incest taboo, 23
Incoherence, 128
Induction, 31
Inertia, 101
Infinity, 96
Inside/outside, 29–30, 118, 122
Integrity, 101, 113, 114, 123, 124
Interférences (intersections), 96
International Psychoanalytic Association,
49, 52, 54, 56
Intersubjectivity, 96–97
Intertextuality, 13
Intrigue, 102
Irigaray, Luce, 54, 57
Irony, 32, 36, 47, 48, 57, 88–92, 112, 119
Isomorphism, 113, 117
Isotopes, 101–102, 118

Jakobson, Roman, xiii, xiv, 1, 4, 7, 8,
10–12, 13, 14, 21, 37, 39, 43, 49, 98,
100, 101, 103, 107, 125
Jambet, Christian, 92, 93
James, William, 129
Jameson, Fredric, 9, 68, 102, 112, 117,
154
Jansenism, 116, 119
Japan, 40
Jewish, 21, 26, 87

Johns Hopkins University, xiv, 41, 115
Johnson, Barbara, 48, 154
Jouissance (erotic pleasure), 46

Kant, Immanuel, 95, 116, 126
King Lear, 59
Kinship studies, 23–24, 123, 134
Klein, Melanie, 58
Klinkenberg, Jean-Marie, 100
Knowledge, 61–74
Kohler, Wolfgang, 6
Kris, Ernst, 51
Kristeva, Julia, 13, 37, 58, 115, 124,
128, 129, 140
Kuhn, Thomas, 60, 72, 73
Kurzweil, Edith, 76

Lacan, Jacques, xiii, xiv, xv, 1, 4, 19, 27,
29, 32, 35, 46, 47–59, 61, 66, 68, 72,
76, 77, 86, 89, 90, 91, 96, 108, 113,
121, 124, 125, 126, 139
Language alliance, 10
Langue (linguistic community), 9, 10,
49–51, 52, 60, 125
Lanser, Susan K., 108
Lanson, Gustave, 36, 38
Lardreau, Guy, 92, 93
Larvatus prodeo, 41–43
Law, 11, 12, 14, 16, 17, 18, 28, 53, 54,
58, 66, 72, 95, 108, 114, 124
Leach, Edmund, 23, 24, 124
Leclaire, Serge, 57
Lefebvre, Henri, 25, 30, 41, 80, 85
Leibnitz, Gottfried, 6, 94, 95, 96, 121
Lenin, Vladimir I., 79, 85
Leowentsein, Rudolf, 51
Lévi-Strauss, Claude, xiii, xiv, 1, 2, 4, 7,
8, 11, 16, 17, 18, 19, 21–31, 33, 34,
35, 38, 41, 47, 48, 61, 62, 64, 73, 76,
77, 78, 79, 83, 90, 91, 99, 105, 108,
109, 112, 113, 114, 115, 116, 121,
122, 123, 124, 125, 126, 129, 134,
135, 136
Levy, Bernard-Henri, 29, 92, 93, 129
Lewis, John, xv, 78, 79, 81, 84
Libidinal economy, 128
Lie, 50, 51, 127